OXFORD PHILOSOPHICAL MONOGRAPHS

Editorial Committee

Michael Dummett, Anthony Kenny
D. H. Rice, Ralph C. S. Walker

FALSE CONSCIOUSNESS

False Consciousness

DENISE MEYERSON

CLARENDON PRESS · OXFORD
1991

Oxford University Press, Walton Street, Oxford OX2 6DP
Oxford New York Toronto
Delhi Bombay Calcutta Madras Karachi
Petaling Jaya Singapore Hong Kong Tokyo
Nairobi Dar es Salaam Cape Town
Melbourne Auckland
and associated companies in
Berlin Ibadan

Oxford is a trade mark of Oxford University Press

Published in the United States
by Oxford University Press, New York

British Library Cataloguing in Publication Data
Data available

Library of Congress Cataloging in Publication Data
Meyerson, Denise.
False consciousness/Denise Meyerson
p. cm.—(Oxford philosophical monographs)
Includes bibliographical references and index.
1. Philosophy of mind. 2. Philosophy, Marxist. 3. Analysis
(Philosophy) I. Title. II. Series.
BD418.3.M49 1991 128'.4—dc20 90-21984
ISBN 0-19-824819-9

Typeset by Cotswold Typesetting Ltd, Cheltenham
Printed in Great Britain by
Biddles Ltd, Guildford & King's Lynn

To my parents

PREFACE

The aim of this book is to provide a philosophical elucidation and defence of the concept of false consciousness. In one way this might seem a problematic enterprise in that the idea is inherited from a tradition, the Marxist tradition, which is not merely vague about the concept but actually divided on the question of its usefulness. But the book is not intended to be a scholarly survey of Marx's or Marxist thought. The aim is to show that there are some interesting claims about certain kinds of irrationality which can be reconstructed from Marxism in a philosophically defensible way. To show this will require a lot of discussion of issues in the philosophy of mind which may be unexpected. It is an unfortunate fact that Marxists tend to be disdainful of orthodox analytic philosophy while analytic philosophers usually assume Marxism to be an impossibly hermetic area not worth cultivating. The truth, though, is that Marx wrote with great insight about phenomena of philosophical interest, and although he frequently did so allusively and suggestively rather than precisely and abstractly, it is analytic philosophy, with its exacting standards of clarity and sensitivity to subtleties, which can help to reveal how compelling Marx's positions are. It would be a reasonable suspicion that there is an emotional or wishful contribution to the beliefs of those in both camps who deny this. I hope this book will not only overcome their mutual dismissiveness but also explain how it is possible for beliefs to be coloured by animus in this way.

ACKNOWLEDGEMENTS

No ordinarily reflective person who lives, as I do, in South Africa can fail to be impressed by the efficacy of ideology, and its overwhelming impact on people's beliefs and attitudes; it is this perception which explains my interest in the topics discussed in this book. I submitted a thesis on the subject for the B.Phil. at Oxford in 1979, and another for the D.Phil. at Oxford in 1987, and I must thank, for their kindness and generous help, my supervisors, Jerry Cohen, Charles Taylor, and especially David Pears, who commented liberally and invaluably on various drafts. I must also mention Sheldon Leader, Michael Nupen, and Jonathan Suzman, my teachers at the University of the Witwatersrand, who introduced me to Marxist social theory and to philosophy; my examiners, Patrick Gardiner and Alan Montefiore, for their encouragement and many useful remarks; an anonymous reader for Oxford University Press for excellent advice; and those who have commented at other times on ideas expressed in this book—Jonathan Bennett, Dick Hare, Mark Leon, Nigel Love, Ian Macdonald, Tom Nagel, Michael Pendlebury, Andrew Prior, Lawrie Reznek, Alan Ryan, Augustine Shutte, and Tom Sorell. I owe a special debt to David Brooks, on whose willingness to discuss philosophy and philosophical knowledge I have frequently relied. But I owe most to my husband, Paul Taylor, who has read and reread everything I have written. The influence of his judgement is everywhere in this book, as in my life.

The Human Sciences Research Council provided generous financial assistance for my research and Liz Carlos efficiently transferred the manuscript onto disk. I am grateful to David Bishop for assistance with the index.

I must record some non-philosophical debts. I thank my parents for their years of support and encouragement. I am grateful to Dr Roger Melvill, whose surgery and care restored my health which suffered a crisis while I was writing this book. It is not the usual exaggeration to say that without him the book would never have been completed. And finally there is our son Max who, by leading me to spend an undreamt-of amount of time in his company, not only compelled me to make diligent use of what remained, but also tutored me in previously unimagined subjects.

CONTENTS

INTRODUCTION   1

  I. PRIMARY AND SECONDARY   17
    1. Forces of Production, Relations of Production, and Superstructure
    2. Causation
    3. 'The Middle Ages could not live upon Catholicism'
    4. Engels
    5. Useful Beliefs Explained by their Usefulness

  II. MISTAKES ABOUT MOTIVES AND MOTIVATED MISTAKES   34
    1. Mistakes about Motives
    2. Some Possibilities
    3. Happy Accidents and Systematic Correlations
    4. Non-rational Causation
    5. Desires and Plans
    6. How Motivated Mistakes are Possible

  III. UNHAPPY DESIRES   70
    1. 'Inhuman, sophisticated, unnatural and imaginary appetites'
    2. Some Theories
    3. True Wants
    4. How do Prudential Considerations Motivate Us?
    5. Facts and Interests
    6. Reasons
    7. A Want-independent Conception of Interests

  IV. ROGUE DESIRES   130
    1. A History for Desires
    2. Some More Qualms about Desires

  V. RECIDIVIST BELIEFS AND DESIRES   146
    1. Cognitive Illusions
    2. Some Examples

Contents

3. Ideological Beliefs
4. The Independence of Desires from Valuations

CONCLUSION   169

REFERENCES   171

INDEX   177

Introduction

Ideology was not a concept treated systematically by Marx and 'false consciousness' was a term never used by him, although he certainly described the phenomenon to which Engels gave that name. His thoughts can be found scattered through various texts which are not even agreed by Marxists to be consistent. But my interests are not scholarly and so there is no need for me to attempt to compile or reconcile the fragments. It will be enough for my purposes to extract some broad themes, remaining faithful, I hope, to the distinctive core of Marx's views without getting caught up in recondite questions of exegesis. The extraction of those themes and the explanation of the philosophical questions they raise will be the tasks of this introduction.

Marx's project, in his early writings, was to show that certain conceptions of religion and politics were misconceived. Feuerbach before him had argued that the idealist philosophy of his time always got things the wrong way round. For instance, it saw God as the subject and man as nothing but his instrument—whereas in reality man is the subject and God merely his projection. Religious dogmas, said Feuerbach, are fantasies which originate in human needs and wishes, in particular in the attempt to compensate for human misery by retreating to the satisfactions of an imaginary world.[1] Marx endorsed these debunking conclusions and went on to apply the same diagnosis, of getting things back to front, to Hegel's theory of the state. Hegel saw *Geist*, or spirit, as the acting subject, and social and political institutions as dictated by it, mere forms of its life-history. But the truth, according to Marx, is that human beings are the real agents and it is human activity which lies behind political institutions. Hegel's view was not merely a mystification, added Marx, but a conservative mystification, because an appearance of legitimacy is inevitably given to

---

[1] See, for instance, David McLellan's chapter on Feuerbach's thought in his *The Young Hegelians and Karl Marx*.

existing political arrangements once they are represented as expressions of the will of a cosmic subject.[2]

In later writings Marx began to look for the source of such mystifications in social conditions. In the fourth of the 'Theses on Feuerbach', for instance, Marx says:

Feuerbach starts out from the fact of religious self-estrangement, of the duplication of the world into a religious world and a secular one. His work consists in resolving the religious world into its secular basis. But that the secular basis lifts off from itself and establishes itself as an independent realm in the clouds can only be explained by the inner strife and intrinsic contradictoriness of this secular basis.[3]

In *The German Ideology*, Marx and Engels went further, explaining that men are social beings and if they and their circumstances appear upside down in all ideology, this is to be explained by the nature of their productive activity and their productive relationships. They called this conception of history 'materialist', saying that it sets out 'from real, active men, and on the basis of their real life-process [demonstrates] the development of the ideological reflexes and echoes of this life-process'.[4] In particular, the fact that through most of history the means of production have been controlled by one class of people but worked by another has given rise to the state as an 'illusory community' and to the political illusion that the ruling class is a servant of communal interests.[5] Later Marx reiterated these materialist claims when he described as the 'guiding thread' of his studies the belief that

in the social production of their life, men enter into definite relations that are indispensable and independent of their will, relations of production which correspond to a definite stage of development of their material productive forces. The sum total of these relations of production constitutes the economic structure of society, the real basis, on which rises a legal and political superstructure, and to which correspond definite forms of social consciousness. The mode of production of material life conditions the social, political and intellectual life process in general.[6]

[2] *Contribution to the Critique of Hegel's Philosophy of Law*, p. 39.
[3] 'Theses on Feuerbach', p. 4.
[4] *The German Ideology*, p. 36.
[5] Ibid. 46–7.
[6] Preface to *A Contribution to the Critique of Political Economy*, pp. 182–3.

The materialist idea is that different modes of economic
activity give rise, somehow, to different sets of ideas. For
instance, to give a characteristic example, where contract
provides the framework for economic activity, where people
are everywhere—to their mutual advantage apparently—bargaining and exchanging in the market-place, political philosophers tend to take their cue from that, and to view society as
an artificial arrangement, like Hobbes's leviathan, which we
devise and into which we contract in order to serve interests
we have outside it. In other words, where economic trans-
actions are based on consent or contract, it is natural for
philosophers to see consent as the foundation of political
authority too, and to think of men and women as pre-
politically self-sufficient creatures who negotiate themselves
out of a state of nature in order the better to protect their life
and property. This too is an illusion, says Marx in the
Grundrisse. 'The individual and isolated hunter and fisherman,
with whom Smith and Ricardo begin, belongs among the
unimaginative conceits of the eighteenth-century Robinson-
ades ... The more deeply we go back into history, the more
does the individual ... appear as dependent, as belonging to a
greater whole.'[7]

I shall say much more, in the next chapter, about all these
concepts—forces of production, relations of production, base,
and superstructure—and about the relationship between the
different elements. For the moment, it is enough to draw
attention to Marx's claim that economic activity is primary
and determines or explains ideology, which is secondary or
derivative.

Marx continued to pursue these themes although, from the
Grundrisse onwards, and especially in *Capital*, he uses the term
'ideology' less, and talks more about the discrepancy between
appearance and essence and about the illusory surface of
economic life. He saw capitalism as an enchanted, topsy-turvy
world and believed a scientific theory was necessary to
penetrate the misleading appearances it generates, and lift the
mystical veil which conceals the true nature of capitalist
society. He argued, for instance, that workers sell their labour

[7] *Grundrisse*, pp. 83–4.

power, not their labour, and that the expression 'value of labour' is as 'imaginary' an expression as the expression 'value of the earth'. Yet, he said,

These imaginary expressions arise ... from the relations of production themselves. They are categories for the phenomenal forms of essential relations. That in their appearance things often represent themselves in inverted form is pretty well known in every science except Political Economy.[8]

He gives other examples, too, of thought in thrall to appearances. Wage workers appear free, but in reality they are forced to work. They are bound to their employers by 'invisible threads'.[9] A commodity is a 'mysterious' thing.[10] It assumes a 'fantastic form'[11] differing from its real one, the appearance of having value independently of human labour. Part of Marx's account here is that the appearances are not merely seductive, but irresistibly so, since, being generated by the economy, they are 'inseparable from'[12] it and will retain their power as long as the economy retains its power. So ideological beliefs cannot be dispelled by reading in Marx that they are false. Theoretical disclosures cannot loosen their grip. Only a change in the mode of production could have that effect.

In none of this is there any mention of false consciousness. It was Engels who introduced that phrase into the Marxist tradition when he wrote, in a famous letter to Mehring,

Ideology is a process accomplished by the so-called thinker consciously, it is true, but with a false consciousness. The real motive forces impelling him remain unknown to him; otherwise it simply would not be an ideological process. Hence he imagines false or seeming motive forces.[13]

Since then it has been a matter for debate among Marxists whether ideological beliefs are necessarily false, or necessarily involve 'false consciousness'. Some writers say that Marx himself gave up the earlier emphasis on ideologies as upside-

---

[8] *Capital*, i. 503.
[9] Ibid. 538.
[10] Ibid. 77.
[11] Ibid. 81.
[12] Ibid. 77.
[13] *Selected Correspondence*, p. 459.

down representations of the world, or mystifications, and that Engels's talk of falsity was therefore regressive. One argument for this conclusion, that ideological beliefs should not be spoken of as false, is that, according to the later Marx, they are not figments of the imagination or the product of confusion. They correctly reflect the way in which society appears to the observer and therefore correspond to reality.[14] A second argument is that ideologies play an important role in our lives; they therefore partially constitute reality and it is impossible to talk of them as illusions.[15] But neither of these claims convinces me. If ideologies correctly reflect experience, that no more shows them to be true than the fact that I truly report having had a *déjà vu* experience shows that I have actually been here before. The point is that its accuracy cannot transform a report of a non-veridical experience into a description of reality. And since, according to Marx, the experiential world is enchanted, the ideological beliefs which match it cannot be true. As far as the second argument is concerned, the fact that a belief has an effect or plays a role cannot show it is true either, for false beliefs can do that too; think of the effect on a wife of the false belief that her husband has a lover. In any event, beliefs, whether true or false, are not a part of the world. The trouble with both these arguments is their implicit idealism, their assumption that the experienced world is the real world or that mental states like beliefs can somehow constitute reality. One would expect Marxists, of all people, to be inhospitable to such ideas. After all, according to Marx, 'neither thoughts nor language in themselves form a realm of their own ... They are only *manifestations* of actual life.'[16]

The false consciousness which Engels described involves a misinterpretation or misunderstanding of motives. Members of the ruling class believe, for instance, that their actions are intended to benefit the poor, when they are not, or that there is nothing they can do for the poor, when there is. Marx

[14] McLellan suggests something like this in his book, *Ideology*, at p. 15, as does J. Seigel, who says that Marx identified the 'world of false appearances' with the 'world of real existence' (*Marx's Fate*, pp. 360–1). See also K. Russell, 'Science and Ideology', p. 193: 'For Marx, appearance and reality are in some important sense the same. Appearance is, after all, part of reality.'

[15] See Thompson, *Studies in the Theory of Ideology*, pp. 5–6.

[16] *The German Ideology*, p. 447.

himself gave many examples of this kind of thing. He reports, for example, that English capitalists of the nineteenth century rationalized their failure to do anything for the poor by an appeal to Malthus's theory that the population always increases at such a rate as to outrun the supply of the means of subsistence. The bourgeoisie concluded that poverty is unavoidable.

The 'principle of population', slowly worked out in the eighteenth century, and then, in the midst of a great social crisis, proclaimed with drums and trumpets as the infallible antidote to the teachings of Condorcet, etc., was greeted with jubilance by the English oligarchy as the great destroyer of all hankerings after human development.[17]

 Part of the idea is that these rationalizations are somehow useful. They are a factor in explaining economic success. In *The German Ideology*, for instance, Marx and Engels claim that each ascendant class has illusions about itself and these illusions are the essential vehicle for its economic aims:

Each new class which puts itself in the place of one ruling before it is compelled, merely in order to carry through its aim, to present its interest as the common interest of all the members of society, that is, expressed in ideal form: it has to give its ideas the form of universality, and present them as the only rational, universally valid ones.[18]

And in *The Eighteenth Brumaire of Louis Bonaparte* Marx explains how grand myths may be mobilized in the service of narrow economic ends:

Unheroic as bourgeois society is, it nevertheless took heroism, sacrifice, terror, civil war and battles of peoples to bring it into being. And in the classically austere traditions of the Roman Republic its gladiators found the ideals and the art forms, the self-deceptions that they needed in order to conceal from themselves the bourgeois limitations of the content of their struggles and to maintain their passion on the high plane of great historical tragedy.[19]

So, in dressing up their passions, members of the ruling class successfully obscure from themselves, and thereby serve, their partisan aims.

---

[17] *Capital*, i. 578, n. 2.
[18] *The German Ideology*, p. 60.
[19] *The Eighteenth Brumaire of Louis Bonaparte*, pp. 104–5.

What is more, since members of the ruling class rule also as 'thinkers, as producers of ideas',[20] their illusions are the ruling illusions and even the members of the subordinate class find them compelling. This means that ruling-class interests are doubly served—for while the bourgeoisie forge ahead, the workers do not resist. In fact, the absence of class consciousness in the working class is another form of false consciousness, according to Marxists. Everyone will know that the proletariat has not proved as insurrectionary as Marx predicted. The standard Marxist explanation of this is that workers have a poor perception of their interests. They have absorbed commercial values and chase after consumer goods. Their desires have been organized by a system which depends on their docility. In short, they suffer from false consciousness. Marcuse is perhaps the most famous exponent of this view. In *One-Dimensional Man* he claims that false consciousness involves taking 'immediate' for 'real' interests,[21] and that people have 'false needs', needs 'superimposed upon the individual by particular social interests in his repression'. Their satisfaction 'serves to arrest the development of the ability . . . to recognize the disease of the whole and grasp the chances of curing the disease'. Examples of these false needs are 'Most of the prevailing needs to relax, to have fun, to behave and consume in accordance with the advertisements, to love and hate what others love and hate'.[22]

There are other contexts, too, in which this idea, that people can have inappropriate desires, has found a congenial home. Feminists, for instance, make use of it to account for female opposition to feminism or for the longing of women to meet the impossible standards of attractiveness set by the media and the fashion world. And it is a commonplace that colonized people do themselves a disservice when they identify with their colonizers, donning a 'white mask'[23] and internalizing the colonial values, attitudes, and aspirations.

Having sketched the background, I am now in a position to explain the concerns of this book. I am interested, in the first

[20] *The German Ideology*, p. 59.
[21] Marcuse, *One-Dimensional Man*, p. xiii.
[22] Ibid. 4–5.
[23] See Fanon, *Black Skin White Masks*.

place, in the twin states of mind which are said to involve false consciousness: first, the rationalizations of members of the ruling class, their inaccurate conception of their motives, and, second, the blindness of the workers to their interests, their identification with the capitalist system. I am also interested in the idea that these mistakes are useful—not necessarily to those who make them, for of course the confusions of the ruled are not useful to them, but to the ruling class. It is the rulers who benefit from both mistakes. The idea is that economic arrangements need to be screened. They would be less stable and function less agreeably if those who have a stake in them did not glamorize their motives and if those who are exploited by them were not blind to their interests. But economic exploitation might need to be screened, and in fact be screened, and yet not be screened because of the need. Marxism, however, makes the latter, explanatory, claim as well, for it asserts, as we have seen, that the economy is primary and explains the character of ideology. It asserts, in other words, that their screening effect is the reason for the mistakes.

I argue in this book that one thing this account implies is an aetiology for the inaccurate beliefs and the inappropriate desires. For it claims they are explained by their advantages and so it is committed to some causal story in virtue of which that is true (see Ch. I. 5). This already puts a certain distance, at the level of theory, between the account of irrationality that a Marxist must provide and the sort of account you get from psychologists who are interested in the faulty inferences people are prone to make. For although psychologists think that bias and error sometimes have useful effects, they do not think that they are necessarily explained by their effects. One of my aims in this book is to supply accounts, compatible with Marxism, of how the ruled might acquire their desires and the rulers their view of their motives.

I canvass three possibilities in the latter case. The first tries to work a 'Darwinian' account. It claims that what is involved is the greater survival value of beliefs which legitimate an economic set-up. It puts to use the insight of psychologists that bias and error, even self-serving bias and error, need not be due to the influence of wishes and emotions on beliefs. This first candidate altogether bypasses the mind. The second candidate goes via the mind, via desire in particular, but bypasses the will. It claims that the beliefs which the Marxist is talking about are directly and automatically affected by desires. Finally, the third candidate implicates the will. It postulates a strategy and claims that members of the ruling class are motivated to see themselves in a certain light. I argue that it is the third theory which a Marxist needs (see Ch. II. 5).

Everyone will see the point of investigating the history of the rationalizations of the ruling class. It is obviously a defect in a belief that it is false and when beliefs are systematically false we expect their history to indicate why. But when it comes to the history of ideological *desires*, to giving an account, compatible with Marxism, of how members of the subordinate class acquire commercial and money values, the question is complicated by the fact that it is not even obvious that desires can suffer from a defect, let alone that there is an obvious defect from which they suffer. But if desires cannot suffer from a defect there is much less point in investigating how people might acquire them. Why bother to investigate the history of ideological desires if it is impossible to point to a way in which they have gone wrong? In Chapter III of this book I argue that that is not impossible. I argue that the fulfilment of our desires does not necessarily make us better off (Ch. III. 7); that what is good for us is a factual matter (Ch. III. 5); and that our desires for ourselves go wrong when they fail to connect with our well-being (Ch. III. 7). And that, of course, is exactly the defect from which the ideological desires are supposed to suffer. For Marxism says that the aspirations of members of the working class are systematically out of touch with their interests. So there is a point in investigating their history for their history ought to explain the divergence. Again I canvass three possibilities, though at less length: a mental contribution on the part of the victims (exaggerating the desirability of the inevitable), deliberate manipulation by the rulers, and, finally, conditioning. I argue that a Marxist needs the third mechanism (Ch. IV. 1).

I have been talking about an implication of the claim that ideological mistakes are derivative and explained by their beneficial effects on the economy, namely that there must be some underlying account, consistent with Marxism, which explains how people come to make the mistakes. Another aspect of the claim that the economy is primary will also be discussed in this book, namely that the ideology is 'inseparable from' the economy and will not be dislodged until there is a change in that; mere exposure to counter-evidence will never be enough. This is a doctrine which looks implausible because philosophers immediately assume that beliefs must respond to evidence, but in fact I think this assumption is wrong. Psychologists and novelists have never doubted that beliefs can be insensitive to reasoning. There is a nice description of the phenomenon in Norman Mailer's *Tough Guys Don't Dance*. Tim Madden says, on learning that his wife is dead, that the thought had 'nothing to offer but its integument. It was like the envelope to a telegram that has no message inside.'[24] Ordinarily, the recognition of evidence is full-blown and brings the message or conviction with it. But sometimes acknowledging and believing evidence can come apart and then acknowledgement, like an envelope which contains nothing, has no effect. I discuss some findings of psychologists in Ch. V. 2.

I have mentioned ideological beliefs and how they are claimed to survive contrary evidence. I also discuss the analogue of this idea for ideological desires, namely that they can continue to motivate an agent who has come to value them negatively and will only lose their grip when there is a change in the economy. If that is true, another everyday assumption is wrong, namely the assumption that desires cannot resist an unconditional negative valuation, valuing and acting being necessarily connected. I argue that this assumption is wrong and that it is in general possible for values and motives to come apart (Chs. III. 4 and V. 4).

I also argue that there is an explanation available to a Marxist for the stubbornness of these beliefs and desires. It relies on the fact that attitudes to property transactions, commercial values, and so on, are so deeply fixed in all our institutions, and experienced as so natural, that the theoretical evidence is disarmed (see Ch. V. 3).

---

[24] Mailer, *Tough Guys Don't Dance*, p. 193.

In fact the concerns of this book are connected and therefore form a cluster. In particular, the fact that the beliefs and desires in question are explained by their usefulness is relevant to the falsity of the beliefs and the inappropriateness of the desires. Take the beliefs. Beliefs are appropriately caused by other beliefs to which they are rationally related. They are inappropriately caused if, even though you think you have a reason for your belief, what actually sustains it is something else. There may be a physicalist account of the belief's origin: you have a brain lesion, or are drugged, or have had your neurons interfered with by a neuro-scientist.[25] Another possibility is that there is a mental cause of the belief, although not one which is rationally related to the belief which is its effect. (I owe this formulation to Donald Davidson[26] and I say more about it later (see Ch. II. 4)). A desire, for instance, is not the right kind of cause for a belief. Nor is it a reason to believe some proposition that it is your duty to believe it.[27] Now the importance of investigating a belief's history is that it bears on the likelihood of its being true: if the belief is true but its causation is eccentric, then it is true by coincidence only. I argue this in Ch. IV. 1. For the moment the point is just that the ideological beliefs of the ruling class about their motives do have an eccentric history. I have given the reason for this: it has to do with the way in which the fact that the beliefs serve economic interests helps to explain them. In particular, there is a motive operating. But if that is so, we can have no general reason for expecting the beliefs to be true. So although a belief which serves class or economic interests is not automatically false, it is not likely to be true either. To summarize: if ideological beliefs occur because they are useful, then they are also likely to be false. So the fact that they serve interests, the fact that they are explained by their serving those interests, and the probable falsity of the beliefs are all connected.

[25] I do not mean to deny that a physicalist account might be available in the case of rational beliefs too, but in their case, though not in the other, it will always be possible—and more likely to be illuminating, even if we were to have the neurophysiological knowledge—to identify the cause of the belief under a mental description, as a piece of reasoning, or a perception.

[26] Davidson, 'Paradoxes of Irrationality', p. 298.

[27] See Cohen, 'Beliefs and Roles', p. 56.

Some writers, especially those who think that there are different 'senses' of 'ideology' in Marx, fail to see the connections here. For instance, it is quite common to distinguish Marx's 'functional' or 'pragmatic' claim about ideology, that ideological beliefs are explained by their tendency to serve ruling-class interests, from his 'epistemological' claim, that ideological beliefs are false. Sometimes the conclusion drawn is that these claims are not necessarily connected. According to Allen Wood, for instance, 'functional ideology need not be ideological illusion. In principle, at least, it seems that historical knowledge, even the doctrine of historical materialism itself, might be functional ideology, that is, it might become influential or socially prevalent because it serves the interests of a class'.[28] Some writers go even further and conclude that one or the other conception should be dropped. Alex Callinicos, for instance, suggests that the epistemological element of Marx's theory of ideology should be scrapped, for once we take seriously the role of ideologies in the class struggle, the question of their truth or falsity is beside the point.[29]

Raymond Geuss is someone who cannot be criticized along these lines, for he does see that there could be connections between the different claims. However, his view of the connections is different from mine. He distinguishes 'epistemic error' from 'non-epistemic error', claiming that beliefs can be false not only in virtue of their epistemic properties, but also in virtue of their functional or genetic properties. According to him, a belief is false in virtue of its functional properties if a subject aware of its function would not accept it. And a belief is false in virtue of its genetic properties if it is accepted for a motive which the subject could not acknowledge.[30] Geuss is at pains to point out that what he means is that the falsity of the belief actually consists in something to do with its origin, not that it is likely to be false in virtue of its origin, because the

[28] Wood, Karl Marx, p. 120.
[29] Callinicos, *Marxism and Philosophy*, p. 135. Joe McCarney finds only the practical conception of ideology in Marx's writings, claiming that for Marx ideological thought is thought which serves class interests, nothing more, its truth or falsity being a matter of indifference. See *The Real World of Ideology*, ch. 3, *passim*.
[30] Geuss, *The Idea of a Critical Theory*, pp. 19–21.

latter would be criticism along ordinary epistemic lines rather than having a non-epistemic dimension.[31] These claims seem to me problematic. First, it certainly does not follow from the fact that I need to be ignorant of the function or origin of a belief of mine, that the belief is false. Suppose an acquaintance of mine is poor at her work, and that I believe she is, but my belief is not based on knowledge of her work. It was formed under the influence of resentment and envy. If I came to know about its origin, I might then cease to hold the belief, but that would not be because the belief is false—as we know, it is not false—but rather because I no longer have a general reason for thinking it true. Second, when the origin of beliefs must be concealed, that is not, as Geuss suggests, because they are accepted for a motive which the subjects could not acknowledge. That is superficial, because the subjects could acknowledge that they have the motive. What they could not acknowledge is that the motive has been at the heart of a campaign to get them to form a desired belief. I say more about this in Ch. II. 6, where I argue that you can acknowledge that you have a motive to believe p; what you cannot acknowledge is that you believe p on account of the motive, that your belief is motivated. But that is for the deeper reason, to be enlarged on there, that intentional activity aimed at producing belief must be ascribed to some sub-system within the mind. Otherwise, I argue, the formation of the irrational belief would be impossible to explain. Third, Geuss does not see that a belief's origin is also likely to be connected with its functional properties, a connection which exists in virtue of the fact that it is usually a deviant or non-standard history which explains the presence of convenient beliefs, or beliefs which serve a function.

Some philosophers have argued that it is a fallacy, the genetic fallacy, to think that the origins of a belief could be relevant to its validity. Origins and validity, they argue, are unconnected issues, where a belief comes from being a matter for sociological or psychological investigation and having nothing whatsoever to do with its justifiability. But I have said that there is a connection between the history of a belief and

[31] Ibid. 38.

its likelihood of being true. Does it then follow from my view that the genetic fallacy is not a fallacy after all? The answer to this question depends on what the fallacy is supposed to be. A popular view is that rational beliefs, being backed up by reasons, cannot be the effect of causes, and that a belief which is caused is therefore unlikely to be true. If it is this view, or something like it, which is supposed to be fallacious, then that is a verdict with which I would agree, for I think that all beliefs, even those which are reliably acquired, have causes. But if the idea behind the genetic fallacy is that no matter what cause a belief has, one can conclude nothing about the likelihood of its being true, then I disagree. For my view is that if a belief has an eccentric causal history, then it is luck if it turns out true.

So much for the connection between the various features of ideological beliefs. As far as the desires are concerned, I argue that there is a parallel connection between how likely a desire is to benefit an agent and its source (see Ch. IV. 1).

It is worth remarking that one theme which unites all these issues is the idea of penetration and non-transparency. Marxism rejects surface explanations. It derides historians who 'take every epoch at its word and believe everything it says and imagines about itself'.[32] It says that experience is misleading and therefore 'conceptions which arise about the laws of production in the minds of agents ... will diverge drastically from these real laws'.[33] It rejects agents' conceptions of what inspires their behaviour and disregards their view of what is good for them. We are in the area of 'real interests' and 'true wants'. One of the aims of this book is to bring clarity to this area, by investigation of the phenomena to which these phrases somewhat ambiguously refer. To give just two examples of the kind of ambiguity I mean : 'real interests' can indicate 'the concerns by which a person ought to be motivated but is not'; used in that way it raises such questions as whether interests are a factual matter and whether they consist in the satisfaction of desires. But the phrase can also mean 'the impulses which really move us, whatever we may think', and then we want to know what the explanation of the

---

[32] *The German Ideology*, p. 62.   [33] *Capital*, iii. 313.

misperception might be. Marx gestures at the first use in *The Holy Family* where, talking about the proletariat's interest in emancipating itself, he says, 'It is not a question of what this or that proletarian, or even the whole proletariat, at the moment *regards* as its aim. It is a question of *what the proletariat is*.'[34] And here is an excerpt from *The Eighteenth Brumaire* in which he uses the phrase in the second way:

as in private life one differentiates between what a man thinks and says of himself and what he really is and does, so in historical struggles one must still more distinguish the language and the imaginary aspirations of parties from their real organism and their real interests, their conception of themselves from their reality.[35]

'True wants' is equally ambiguous. It can mean 'the desires which really motivate an agent', in which case it does the same work, and raises the same questions, as the use of 'real interests' in the excerpt from *The Eighteenth Brumaire*. But some have taken it to mean 'desires whose fulfilment makes the agent better off', and about that use it is legitimate to ask whether it makes sense of the concept of desire. All of these issues are discussed in this book: on facts and interests see Ch. III. 5; whether interests are want-based or not is discussed in Ch. III. 7; possible explanations of people's inaccurate conception of themselves are examined in Ch. II. 2; finally, for investigation of the claim that what you truly want is what is good for you, see Ch. III. 3.

The upshot, I hope, of these and other parts of the book, will be to show that certain deep kinds of irrationality are possible: that people are not necessarily the best judges of their interests, that they can make motivated mistakes about their characters, and that beliefs can be tenacious and held against the weight of what is taken to be good evidence. These conclusions bear out some claims of Marxists. They should also appeal to other political groupings, people who, though not Marxists, believe that vested interests can play a role in explaining beliefs and that forces like conditioning can get in the way of and frustrate a true perception of interests. Feminists are an obvious example. More than that, they should

---

[34] *The Holy Family*, p. 37.
[35] *The Eighteenth Brumaire of Louis Bonaparte*, p. 128.

interest anyone intrigued by the complex nature of out-of-the-ordinary mental states and who believes that people can have a false picture of their characters and their behaviour. Much that is psychologically interesting goes on below the surface. That is a theme of this book.

I

Primary and Secondary

1. FORCES OF PRODUCTION, RELATIONS OF PRODUCTION, AND SUPERSTRUCTURE

What is primarily of importance in any human society is, according to Marx, the nature of its forces of production or its productive forces. These are the labour power, the materials, and the instruments and tools used in the process of production. 'Corresponding' to these forces of production, at any rate in stable situations, are certain economic relations or relations of production. They are the relationships of power and control which are appropriate to the operation of the productive forces. Serfdom, for instance, is better suited to some methods of production than others. Class is a function of position in this network of social organization and domination, a network which constitutes, according to Marx, the economic structure or real basis of society and also 'determines' its law, its politics, its religion, its morality, and its ideology—determines, in short, everything labelled by Marx superstructural.[1] But what exactly does that mean? In what sense could the economic structure of society determine,

[1] I do not expect that my summary of Marx's beliefs will be acceptable to all Marxist scholars. For instance, not everyone will agree with me that Marx made technology the most fundamental factor in history, nor that the forces of production are part of the base, nor that ideology is part of the superstructure. Richard Miller, for example, argues against a technological determinist reading of Marx in the fifth chapter of his book. *Analyzing Marx*: Jon Elster claims that in the base are located both the relations of production and the productive forces (*An Introduction to Karl Marx*, p. 104); and G. A. Cohen claims that the superstructure does not strictly speaking include ideology, although much that is true of the superstructure is also true of ideology (*Karl Marx's Theory of History*, p. 216). I shall not pursue these issues. In the first place, exegesis would take me too far from the aims of this book, and secondly, the problems dealt with in this chapter in any event transcend the particular view one has of the constitution of base and super-structure, for the question of how to interpret the claim that ideology is derivative or determined arises whatever view one takes of the nature of the elements of historical materialism.

among other things, its ideology? The next chapter of this book assumes a particular interpretation of that notoriously elusive formulation; the task of this chapter will be to explain why that interpretation is most appealing. It is intended as a relatively brief preliminary, an explanation of the attractions of a particular view of Marx's thought, in preparation for the argument of the next chapter. Four possible reasons for ascribing a determining role to the economic base will be canvassed:

(*a*) that the nature of the economic relationships in which people stand causes certain ideological beliefs to be dominant;

(*b*) that their standing in economic relationships is a necessity of life, and therefore a necessary prerequisite for everything else less basic;

(*c*) that their economic relationships are, if not the only, at least the 'ultimate' cause of their beliefs; and

(*d*) that their beliefs are explained by their suitability to the current set of economic relationships.

The superiority of the last of these interpretations will be explained.

2. CAUSATION

Probably the most obvious way to construe Marx's materialist claim is to suppose that he meant that the economic structure of society and the dominant ideology are related as ordinary cause and effect; indeed, the best-known objections to historical materialism assume that that is all he could have meant. I shall start with these objections and investigate how workable they are. The upshot will be that one of them, at any rate, succeeds, thus revealing the untenability of Marx's claim, if he meant it causally.

According to Acton, the materialist conception of history claims that economic factors have a causal agency, and he argues against this that economic factors could only play such a role if the elements of the conception were 'distinguishable'. But, he says, they are not: the economic structure of society is not distinguishable from the legal, moral, and political relationships of men. For productive relationships or relations of production involve rules which allow for the efficient operation of productive forces. No one would dig if the crops were constantly trampled down, for instance, and no one would go fishing if the trawlers were liable to be confiscated.[2] But these rules that allow production to continue peaceably 'comprise' moral, customary, and legal relationships and therefore 'are' moral, legal, and political.[3] Moral, legal and political relationships are therefore, Acton says, 'aspects' of the productive relationships.[4] Later he adds that it is not fanciful to regard law, morals, and politics as 'parts' of the means of production. 'For good laws, good morals and good government can help production, as bad laws, bad morals and bad government can hinder it.'[5]

Plamenatz makes similar claims. He argues that morality, custom, and law, in the broad sense of rules which impose obligations and confer rights, are 'involved in' all kinds of social activity and therefore cannot be caused by any aspect of social life, economic or otherwise.[6]

G. A. Cohen criticizes this use of the notion of involvement, saying that e can both involve and cause f,[7] and that seems right. The trouble with Plamenatz's view is that involvement is such a vague concept that it is hard to know what it rules out. Certainly it does not, on the face of it, exclude causation, for if an action causes an effect, there is a natural sense in which the effect is involved with the action. However, it is not quite fair to say that Plamenatz does not ever tell us what concept of involvement he has in mind. In fact, he seems to intend it in two different ways. First, he points out that whenever Marx comes to explain the concept of the relations of production, he represents them as property relations or relations of ownership. Ownership of labour power or ownership of machines, for instance, are said by Marx to be relations of production. But that means, says Plamenatz, that economic

---

[2] Acton, *The Illusion of the Epoch*, p. 162.
[3] Ibid. 164–5.
[4] Ibid. 165.
[5] Ibid. 167.
[6] Plamenatz, *Man and Society*, ii. 283–5.
[7] Cohen, 'Being, Consciousness and Roles', in *History, Labour, and Freedom*, pp. 41–2.

relations are *defined* by Marx in terms of the normative claims which individuals make upon each other and recognize. They are defined, in other words, in terms of the legal, moral, and ideological apparatus they are supposed to explain. The explanatory claim must therefore fail, concludes Plamenatz: the economic relationships in which people stand, being normative in character, cannot be said to be the cause or the foundation of that aspect of social life.[8] Second, Plamenatz argues that law, morality, and custom profoundly *affect* economic relations. He points out, for instance, that different customs governing the inheritance of property in land will have different effects on economic activity, and that one system of property as compared with another may lead to much greater productivity by concentrating wealth in fewer hands; he concludes that there is therefore no point in calling the relations of production the real foundation of law and government and all forms of social consciousness.[9]

One thing to notice is that both Acton and Plamenatz tend to muddle these points, slipping between the claim about the description or characterization of productive relationships (productive relationships are characterized normatively) and the claim about the effect of the putatively determined on the putatively determining element (rules about rights and duties affect the relations of production). And although both points are supposed to exclude causation, it is not even clear that they can both be true. But I shall come to that possibility later. For the moment I shall deal with them separately, taking the one about characterization first.

The idea is that because the economic structure of a society is specified in terms of the rights over persons and property recognized in that society, the economic structure cannot be the cause of the legal and ideological edifice. But why should that be so? Why should the fact that beliefs about rights and duties enter into the characterization of the economic structure rule out the possibility that they are caused by the economic structure? The assumption must be that cause and effect have to be identified in logically independent ways. For if they did not have to be identified independently, it would not be relevant that the relations of production are specified in terms of normative claims. But in fact it can be shown that that assumption is false.

There is a well-known argument in the area of philosophy of action which makes the same false assumption. It is to the effect that the relationship between reasons for actions and actions cannot be causal because it is analytic that if you want *F* all things considered, and believe that *G*-ing is the best way to achieve *F*, you *G*.[10] The trouble with this argument is that even if there is a 'logical connection' between the reason for the action and the action, it does not follow that the reason cannot be the cause of the action. For, as Donald Davidson has shown, true causal statements can be analytic. Consider the statement, 'the cause of the accident caused the accident'. Although analytically true, it mentions distinct events which are related as cause and effect.[11] The point is that causality is a relationship between events, not descriptions. It is a relationship between events no matter how they are described.[12] So if events are causally related, substituting different descriptions of the events cannot affect the truth of the causal statement: if '*e* caused *f*' is true, it will remain true no matter how *e* and *f* are described. Once we make the distinction that Davidson makes, between causes and the features we select for describing them, it is clear that the first of Plamenatz's and Acton's arguments cannot succeed, drawing, as it does, a conclusion about what can cause what from a fact about how we talk. Logically independent descriptions are not necessary for causal statements.

But perhaps Plamenatz and Acton could try to improve their argument, replying like this: 'It is true that we can make causal statements without logically independent descriptions.

[10] Naturally, those who assert the claim rely on standard provisos: that *G* is possible for you, physically and psychologically; that if there is a lapse of time between your forming the desire and the opportunity for action, your desire has remained constant; and that you know you are able to *G*. Cf. Taylor, *The Explanation of Behaviour*, p. 38.

[11] 'Suppose', Davidson says, '"*A* caused *B*" is true. Then the cause of *B* = *A*; so substituting, we have "The cause of *B* caused *B*", which is analytic' ('Actions, Reasons and Causes', in *Essays on Actions and Events*, p. 14).

[12] Davidson, 'Mental Events', in *Essays on Actions and Events*, p. 215.

But logically independent descriptions must at least be available. The only reason you can make a true causal statement with "The cause of the accident caused the accident" is because you can describe the cause of the accident in some other way than as "the cause of the accident"—as "the failure of the car's brakes", for instance. And that is also why desires and beliefs can be causes of actions. It is possible to redescribe the desires and beliefs as neuro-physiological events and the actions as muscular contractions. So, although true causal statements can be analytic, it must still be logically possible for cause and effect to occur without each other. That is what Hume meant when he said that causation presupposes logically distinct existences, and where that desideratum is not met the causal relation cannot obtain. For instance, a man's failure to marry could not be the *cause* of his bachelorhood. But,' the reply continues, 'it is just this requirement which is not met in the case of historical materialism. The elements which are supposed by it to be causally related cannot occur without each other. The relations of production did not merely happen to be described in normative language by Marx. They are not different from or separate from normative practices and it therefore follows that they cannot be the cause of them.' Something like this could be behind Acton's claims that economic relationships comprise moral, legal, and political relationships, and that the latter are aspects and parts of the former. For it could be argued that if *f* is part of *e*, then *e* and *f* cannot occur without each other and *e* therefore cannot cause *f*.

But even this improved version of the argument does not work against a causal reading of historical materialism. The reason is that logically independent descriptions of its elements can in fact be provided. Cohen argues this for legal relations on the one hand and productive relations on the other, showing that it is possible to provide a description of productive relations purged of any reference to legal concepts such as property or ownership. Cohen explains that if Marx did not use the sanitized vocabulary, that is just because it is both more cumbrous and more impoverished than the much richer system which operates in terms of property concepts. Briefly, Cohen argues as follows. First he points out that ownership of an object involves rights over that object. For instance, workers' ownership of their labour power is their enjoyment of a right to dispose of it as they wish; ownership of the means of production by capitalists gives them rights in the means of production. Then he argues that for any ownership right we can formulate a power which matches it. For instance, the right to withhold labour is matched by the power to withhold labour. This is not to say that wherever there exists a right, there exists a corresponding power, nor that wherever there exists a power there exists a right. Usually a right guarantees a power, but there are circumstances in which relations of domination are not backed up by legal forms and then Marxism predicts they will be entrenched in other ways—by brute force, perhaps. But the way in which the relations of economic power are sustained is in any event a matter of the *effect* of the legal system and other non-economic institutions on the relations of production, and has nothing to do with Cohen's point, which is that although it is more convenient to talk in *de jure* terms of property, it is more accurate to say that the economic structure is composed of relations of *de facto* economic power, or non-normatively defined abilities to command and dispose of labour and the means of production.[13] As I said, Cohen is specifically concerned to expel legal elements from the definition of the relations of production, but it is clear that the solution could be extended to cover all normative intrusions into economic relations, including, naturally, the moral and customary rules and conventions which Plamenatz thinks so problematic for historical materialism.

To recap: I have been dealing with Plamenatz's and Acton's objection to historical materialism, that the economic structure cannot causally explain law, morality and ideology, because economic relations are characterized in terms of normative concepts, or, on the improved version, are not separate from normative relations. And I argued that their objection is wrong. If their point is that the economic structure cannot be the cause of law, morality, and ideology

---

[13] Cohen, *Karl Marx's Theory of History*, ch. 8. For those who, like Steven Lukes, still doubt whether it is possible to have relations of power without norms (see 'Can the Base be Distinguished from the Superstructure', pp. 113–16), attention to the powers exercised in the animal kingdom may prove Cohen's point.

because it is specified in terms of legal, moral, and ideological concepts, it is wrong because true causal statements can be analytic. If their point is that the economic structure cannot be the cause of those aspects of social life because it is undefinable apart from them, it is wrong because economic relations are a function of what actions are in the economic actors' power, not of what actions their legal and moral practices and ideological beliefs justify.

I come now to Plamenatz's and Acton's second argument which will turn out to fare better. This second argument, it will be remembered, was that the economic structure cannot be the cause of everything non-economic, because law, government, religion, ideology, and all the other influences called superstructural by Marx profoundly affect the economic structure. This has often been represented as an embarrassment for Marxism, for it certainly does seem as though there is a formidable political, legal, and intellectual influence on economic relations, and such an influence would indeed be a barrier to the elements of historical materialism being related as cause and effect. The point is that for a causal reading of historical materialism to succeed, it would at least have to be true that the relations of production play a greater causal role with respect to the superstructure than the superstructure plays with respect to these relations. But the facts seem to suggest that that is not the case. In fact, Marxism itself—indeed, Marxism especially—is committed to the belief that the superstructure greatly affects the relations of production, for, according to Marxists, law, morality, ideological beliefs, and so on entrench and preserve the economic relations. The whole idea is that class relations and exploitation depend for their survival on the legitimating effect of the norms. Ideology, for instance, is said to obscure or screen the true nature of economic relationships, thereby oiling their operation. It is a sort of social cement. To give just one of Marx's examples: the 'mystified' view of classical political economy, that labour has value, extinguishes the difference between necessary and surplus labour, or the fact that workers work part of the time for nothing. The result is that unpaid labour appears as paid and the fact of exploitation is concealed.[14] But if Marxism itself

---

[14] *Capital*, i. 505.

postulates at least as great a causal influence going the other way, from superstructure to economic structure, it follows that a causal reading of historical materialism *must* fail.

I want to conclude this section by pointing out a dilemma for Plamenatz and Acton. I have so far taken the merits and demerits of their two arguments separately, on the assumption that they could both be true. But are they in fact compatible? This question is complicated by the fact that there are two versions of the first argument, the one about the characterization of economic relationships, and that complication in the question needs accommodating in the answer. For it is possible that the two arguments might be compatible if the one about characterization is taken in the improved way, but not in the unimproved way.

I shall start with the first version of the characterization argument, which is that the economic structure is specified in terms of superstructural concepts. Is that compatible with the other argument, that the superstructure profoundly affects the economic structure? Anyone who thought this version of the characterization argument problematic for a causal reading of historical materialism would have to believe that logically independent descriptions are indispensable for causal statements. But someone who believed that could not at the same time make the *other* point, that what was supposed to be the effect actually affects what was supposed to be the cause. For such a person believes that the fact that we talk in a certain way rules out causation *tout court*. So the question about the direction of the causation simply cannot arise. It cannot be part of this view, in other words, that there is a causal influence going in a different way from the way that a causal reading of Marxism would predict. I argued, of course, following Davidson, that nothing follows about whether events are related as cause and effect from the words we use for describing them. So it could be objected that, on the correct account of the matter, someone could put forward both arguments, that the economic structure is specified in superstructural terms, and that the superstructure affects the economic structure. But although that is so, it cannot help Plamenatz and Acton. For if Davidson's account is accepted, then we cannot tell anything about whether there is or is not a causal influence at work from the fact that the economic structure is characterized in non-economic terms. But that means that the characterization argument is vacuous. Plamenatz and Acton are therefore faced with a dilemma: either something substantial does follow from the fact that the economic structure is specified in superstructural terms, but then their other point, about the causal role of the super-structure, cannot be made; or nothing interesting follows from it, but then there is no reason to assert it, and only the other point remains. Either way, one of the arguments goes.

But what of the improved version of the first argument, which says that the economic structure and superstructure are not separate from each other? Is that compatible with the argument about the causal role of the superstructure? Again it seems not. The question as to whether what a Marxist says does the causing really does the causing cannot arise if the improved version of the argument is accepted. For if the economic relations and superstructure cannot occur without each other, it must be the case that *neither* can causally affect the other. You could put this the other way round too, and say that just because the superstructure does have an effect on economic relations, it must be different from those relations.

3. 'THE MIDDLE AGES COULD NOT LIVE UPON CATHOLICISM'

I have argued that the causal understanding of historical materialism, in requiring that the relations of production should affect the superstructure more than the superstructure affects those relations, requires too much. Marx suggests another understanding in *Capital* but it does not imply enough. Apparently a critic had objected to his theory that,

as regards the contemporary world, where material interests are supreme, what [Marx] said was true enough. In the modern world it was true that the special method of production which prevailed, and the appropriate relations of production—in a word, the economic structure of society—formed the real basis on which the juridical and political superstructure were erected, and to which specific social forms of consciousness corresponded. It was true of the modern world that there the method by which the material necessaries of life were produced, determined the general characteristics of social, political and intellectual life. But this did not apply to the Middle Ages, when Catholicism held sway; and it did not apply to ancient Greece and ancient Rome, where political considerations were dominant.

Marx replies as follows:

This much, at any rate, is certain, that the Middle Ages could not live upon Catholicism, nor yet classical antiquity upon politics. On the contrary, the way in which during classical antiquity and the Middle Ages (respectively), people gained a livelihood explained why, in the former case politics, and in the latter case Catholicism, played the leading role.[15]

The fatal difficulty with this, pointed out by Cohen, is in seeing how Marx's unexceptionable claim about the dependence of life on gaining a livelihood could possibly be relevant to the truth of historical materialism. Production of the means of subsistence is necessary to continued life, it is true; but it does not follow that it therefore explains everything non-economic. After all, there are lots of necessary conditions of staying alive other than the production of the means of subsistence, various ways we must look after ourselves, but no reason to think that they have anything to do with the 'general characteristics of social, political and intellectual life'. So the fact that we must produce to live is far too weak to provide support for the desired conclusion, that it is how we produce that explains why it is here religion, and there politics, that plays the 'leading role'.[16]

4. ENGELS

The construal of determination as causation rules out the impressive effect of the superstructure on the economy and therefore rules out too much. But the appeal to what is necessary to survive does not exclude enough. Engels made a

---

[15] Ibid. 56–7, n. 1. The reference in this case is to the Everyman edn. where the translation is less clumsy.

[16] See Cohen, 'On An Argument for Historical Materialism', in *History, Labour, and Freedom*, pp. 127–8.

famous and influential attempt to formulate the relationship between base and superstructure in a way which steers between these, but it is notoriously vague. He says, in a letter to Bloch, that 'the production and reproduction of real life' is not the only but merely 'the *ultimately* determining element' in history. 'The economic situation is the basis, but the various elements of the superstructure . . . also exercise their influence upon the course of the historical struggles.'[17] Again, to Schmidt, he claims that ideology 'reacts in its turn upon the economic basis and may, within certain limits, modify it'.[18] Marxists have often been attracted by these ideas. It is frequently claimed that the base is determinant only in the last instance, while the superstructure is said to have a degree of efficacy, to be 'relatively autonomous', and to be able itself to react back upon the base.

It is easy to see Engels's problem. He wanted to retain the notion of causation by the base but dilute the thesis of its primacy. His solution was to say that the causation is only 'ultimate'. But it is not clear that a sort of watered-down causation is possible. In fact, it seems that if we continue to talk in causal terms there are only two possibilities. Either we opt for a backwards and forwards reciprocal influence model, saying that things economic affect things non-economic and vice versa. But then the distinctiveness of historical materialism is lost, and all we are left with is the mundane view that historical events are caused by a host of factors—political, legal, ideological, economic, and so on. That piece of common sense is not the sort of belief which Marx could have described as the 'guiding thread' of his studies. Or we are forced to claim that the economic structure plays a greater causal role than the superstructure in historical developments. But one thing that vitiates this reading is, as Ted Honderich points out, that it requires something difficult to supply, namely effective principles of counting for particular relations and superstructural elements.[19] Indeed, it could be added that even principles of counting would not be enough, for we would also need some way of quantifying the importance of each relation

[17] *Selected Correspondence*, p. 640.
[18] Ibid. 646.
[19] Honderich, 'Against Teleological Historical Materialism', p. 454.

and each superstructural element. In any event we know already that the claim that the economic structure affects the superstructure more than vice versa is incompatible with the fact that Marxism itself accords at least as great a causal role to the superstructure, namely that of stabilizing the relations of production.

5. USEFUL BELIEFS EXPLAINED BY THEIR USEFULNESS

The problem for historical materialism is this: it claims that the economic structure determines or explains the character of the superstructure, but it is obvious, and indeed insisted on by Marxism, that the economic structure is affected by the superstructure. The problem is to combine explanatory primacy with the huge causal effect of the derivative on the primary factor.

Cohen, in his *Karl Marx's Theory of History: A Defence*, provides a way to combine these. Historical materialism asserts that the superstructure is explained by the base, and Cohen argues that for that assertion to be consistent with the acknowledged role of the superstructure, the idea must be that the super-structure is explained by the effect it is disposed to have on the base: the superstructure is as it is because it tends to have a stabilizing effect on the base. In other words, superstructural institutions have the character they do because the relations of production require that they have that character. It will be remembered that when I discussed the issue of the separate-ness of legal relations from the relations of production, I said that legal rights are usually behind the exercise of economic power; people are able to exercise the powers they do because they have the rights they have. In other words, the legal system *affects* the economy. But that is quite compatible with the explanatory primacy of the economy if you interpret it in teleological terms, saying that the legal system obtains *because* it is disposed to have that effect on the economy, because, in other words, it tends to secure the relations of production. Likewise, the idea is that the character of ideological beliefs and preconceptions is explained by the fact that ideas of that character are disposed to sustain the structure of economic power.[20] Here we have exactly that combination I said was necessary: the explanatory primacy of the relations of production and the efficacy of the superstructure, the superstructure's presence being explained by its effect on the relations of production, namely, that it sustains them. The explanatory primacy of the base, once it is understood teleologically rather than in standard causal terms, *implies* that the superstructure affects the base.

But has the character of superstructural institutions really been explained? According to Cohen, we explain the occurrence of *e* by citing a dispositional fact about it, namely that if it occurs it brings about *f.* Roughly: $(e \rightarrow f) \rightarrow e$. But it might be asked how it could ever be an explanation of something that it has a disposition to produce a certain effect. It is exactly that kind of reasoning that Voltaire justly parodies in *Candide.* Dr Pangloss says: this would be suitable for this, therefore it's there. Noses would be useful for wearing spectacles, therefore noses appear. The absurdity of that shows that the dispositional fact $(e \rightarrow f)$ cannot explain *e*.

The answer to this is that what Dr Pangloss cannot provide, and what has to be present if the dispositional fact is to explain, is an underlying causal account which explains how *e*'s disposition to have a certain effect explains the occurrence of *e*. In general, it could not be a brute fact that something's being beneficial explains its occurrence. If a teleological explanation is legitimate, that is because there exists an answer to the question, 'How does the benefit explain the occurrence?', the existence of such an answer making the difference between a happy accident and a set-up explained by its advantages. So when historical materialism claims that the current ideology does not just conveniently happen to entrench the economic position of the ruling class but prevails *because* of that effect, then it is committed to some supplementary causal account of how the fact that the beliefs confer that benefit explains why they are held.[21]

The upshot is that if there is such an account, it is legitimate for a Marxist to cite their effect on the economy in order to

---

[20] Cohen, *Karl Marx's Theory of History*, ch. 9.

[21] Cohen calls the supplementary causal account an 'elaboration'. See *Karl Marx's Theory of History*, p. 271.

explain the character of ideological beliefs. But what kind of explanation would it be? In *Karl Marx's Theory of History*, Cohen says it is a functional explanation. However, in a later paper, 'Functional Explanation, Consequence Explanation and Marxism', he argues that explanations of the structure defended in his book may or may not be functional explanations. He now prefers to call the explanations to which he argues Marxism is committed 'consequence explanations', so as not to prejudge the issue as to what the relation is between Marxist and functional explanations.[22] There are some advantages in sticking to that and avoiding the question as to whether the explanations of the structure that Cohen describes are or are not functional explanations. In a functional explanation, at any rate as it is usually understood, something is explained by its function. In Cohen's explanations, something is explained by its consequences. More accurately, a dispositional fact about *e*, that if it occurs it brings about *f*, explains the occurrence of *e*.

Why avoid the question as to whether explanations of this structure are or are not the same as functional explanations? First, because if they are not, there is no need for Marxism to defend functional explanations as well as these; and if they are, it will be defending them anyway—just under a different name.

Second, it is arguable, according to Cohen, that they are different, for Darwinism appears to provide consequence but not functional explanations. Here is a consequence explanation which Darwin's theory sustains: the acquisition by giraffes of long necks is explained by the dispositional fact that, because the environment is filled with high trees, long necks would benefit giraffes. But what functional explanation does it sustain? Suppose that some feature *F* is functional for a particular organism *a*. On Darwin's theory, *a* does not have *F* because *F* is functional for *a*. *a* has *F* by chance, or because *F* was functional for past organisms, which consequently had a greater chance of surviving long enough to reproduce than organisms which lacked *F*. If *F* was functional for past organisms, does this explain why *a* has it? Clearly, yes; but it also

[22] Cohen, 'Functional Explanation, Consequence Explanation and Marxism', p. 36.

explains *a*'s having it even if *F* has ceased to be functional for *a*, a change in the environment having made the feature functionless or even dysfunctional for *a*. So Darwin's theory explains features which are functionless and dysfunctional as well as features which are functional. Its explanations cannot therefore be functional explanations—not, at any rate, if functional explanations are explanations of features which are functional.[23]

I have been talking about the advantages of avoiding the issue of functional explanation and it remains to mention one more, which is that the notion of a function carries a lot of luggage along with it. In particular, it is complicated by the question as to whether function-statements are merely some kind of benefit-statement—in which case to attribute a function to some feature *F* is merely to point to some beneficial effect of *F*, regardless of whether *F*'s presence is explained by that effect—or whether function-statements are rather intrinsically explanatory. Larry Wright takes the latter view, arguing that you cannot even talk of something's having a function unless it is explained by its function, that it is part of the meaning of the word 'function' that there is this explanatory extra.[24] This whole debate is really only adventitiously related to the issues that Marxism raises and we can bypass it. The benefit-statements which Marxism makes are in any case explanatory, for theoretical reasons having to do with its account of history. We can avoid all these questions by not calling ideological beliefs functional, and in future I shall speak of them simply as useful or beneficial.

One last point on Cohen's theory: Jonathan Bennett points out that there is a constraint which any theory of teleological explanation must meet. It must show how it can be explanatory to refer to a time later than that of the event to be explained without implying that the later occurrence explains the earlier one. That would be 'backwards causation', efficient causation but with the order reversed, the effect *per impossibile* explaining the cause.[25] Cohen's account satisfies Bennett's requirement admirably by making it the case that what is

---

[23] Cohen, 'Functional Explanation . . . and Marxism', 37–41.
[24] Wright, *Teleological Explanations*, p. 81.
[25] Bennett, *Linguistic Behaviour*, pp. 36–7.

doing the explaining is not the resulting effect but rather a previously existing disposition: the disposition, given the situation, for the superstructure to have a stabilizing effect. A similar analysis applies to the biological example mentioned earlier. The fact that, because of the high trees, long necks are disposed to benefit giraffes explains why giraffes acquired long necks. It is not the resulting benefit which explains the length of the necks. The length is explained by a previously existing propensity: the propensity, given the nature of the environment, for long necks to confer a benefit on giraffes. So consequence explanations are not efficient causal explanations reversed. Instead the occurrence of an event is explained by the dispositional fact that, were it to occur, it would have a certain consequence.[26]

*

I have tried to show in this chapter that the best way to understand the determination of ideological beliefs by economic relationships, while also remaining faithful to that other crux of Marxism, the serviceability of ideology to those in positions of economic power, is to see ideological beliefs as explained by their serviceability. In the next chapter I shall discuss one ramification of this solution.

[26] Cohen, *Karl Marx's Theory of History*, pp. 258–63; 'Functional Explanation, Consequence Explanation and Marxism', pp. 47–8.

II

Mistakes about Motives and Motivated Mistakes

1. MISTAKES ABOUT MOTIVES

We know that Marx and Engels refused to set much store by
the explanations of their behaviour that social actors are
inclined to offer, preferring to look behind the actor's version
and swap for it their very different account. Peel and Cobden,
for instance, explained their support for the repeal of the
Corn Laws by claiming they were motivated by the benevolent
desire that the poor should pay less for their bread. But Marx
and Engels claimed that the explanation lay, rather, in the
interest of industrialists in paying less for the poor.[1] In *The
German Ideology*, along the same lines, they belittle historians
who succumb to the 'illusion of the epoch' in accepting its
opinion that it is 'actuated by purely "political" or "religious"
motives, although "religion" and "politics" are only forms of its
true motives'.[2] For Marx and Engels members of the ruling
class are everywhere dressing up their real motives in more
respectable clothing and, what is equally important, fooling
themselves with the disguise. It is a case of the wolf believing it
is a sheep. Add to this the fact that the illusions of the ruling
class about itself are a factor in its economic success and we
have the whole picture. The bourgeoisie think they are dis-
interested when they really are interested, and their interests
are well served by that failure to see them at work. Roughly,
people who are blind to the exploitative nature of their
activities make better exploiters.

There are many examples of this kind of phenomenon, not
only within the body of Marx's writings. Quentin Skinner, for

---

[1] See, for instance, Engels's letter to Marx of 6 August 1852 (*Collected Works*,
xxxix).

[2] *The German Ideology*, p. 55.

instance, describes how Elizabethan entrepreneurs began to use the word 'religious' to describe punctual, strict, and conscientious forms of behaviour. In thus appropriating the word for the way in which they went about their commercial activities they managed, as Skinner says, to legitimate an economic set-up by an appeal to the most highly approved moral and spiritual values.[3] From Beatrice Webb we have this nice account of her mother's meticulously self-serving beliefs:

Her intellect told her that to pay more than the market rate, to exact fewer than the customary hours or insist on less than the usual strain—even if it could be proved that these conditions were injurious to the health and happiness of the person concerned—was an act of self-indulgence, a defiance of nature's laws which would bring disaster on the individual and the community. Similarly, it was the bounden duty of each citizen to better his social status; to ignore those beneath him, and to aim steadily at the top rung of the social ladder. Only by this persistent pursuit by each individual of his own and his family's interest would the highest general level of civilization be attained.[4]

Naturally novelists, too, give us wonderful examples of such things. There is Nadine Gordimer's Mehring, the protagonist of *The Conservationist*, who transforms his desire to conserve his racial privileges into a kind of sober insight into the futility of change and the sentimentality of the 'pretty women and school boys' who want it.[5] And think of Lady Marchmain's thoughts on wealth, related by Charles Ryder in *Brideshead Revisited*:

'When I was a girl we were comparatively poor, but still much richer than most of the world, and when I married I became very rich. It used to worry me, and I thought it wrong to have so many beautiful things when others had nothing. Now I realise that it is possible for the rich to sin by coveting the privileges of the poor . . .'
    I said something about a camel and the eye of a needle and she rose happily to the point.
    'But of *course*,' she said, 'it's very unexpected for a camel to go through the eye of a needle, but the gospel is simply a catalogue of

[3] Skinner, 'Language and Social Change', p. 570.
[4] B. Webb, *My Apprenticeship*, quoted in D. Miller, 'Ideology and the Problem of False Consciousness', p. 446.
[5] Gordimer, *The Conservationist*, p. 79.

unexpected things. It is not to be *expected* that an ox and an ass should worship at the crib.'[6]

This is the phenomenon which Engels called 'false consciousness' and its analysis will be the subject of this chapter. Of course, there is also, according to Marxism, an accomplice to it, namely the fact that the people who do not have a stake in the status quo take up and accept the self-definitions of those who do. But that will be the subject of discussion later. For the moment the topic is the reassuring picture of their motives from which members of the ruling class profit.

2. SOME POSSIBILITIES

The Marxist account contains two explicit elements. The first is that members of the ruling class do believe what they profess to believe. It is a mistake they make, not a lie they tell. The real motives which are thus camouflaged are hidden as much from them as from outsiders who accept at face value their self-portrayals. The second element is that it is a useful mistake: in legitimating their activities it consolidates the economic arrangements from which they profit. The bulk of the argument in this chapter aims to show that if this account is to be coherent, then a third element has to be introduced into it, and that is a motive. It will be argued, in other words, that the workability of the Marxist thesis about mistaken motives depends on there being a motive for the mistake. And in the last section of the chapter I shall explain how motivated mistakes are possible.

Clearly, from just the fact that the belief about motives is false, nothing follows about its being motivated. For one thing, it is possible that the subjects simply have not got the intellectual skills for arriving at the truth. Perhaps they are bad at collecting or interpreting evidence. Another possibility is that, although the false belief cannot be ascribed to intellectual incompetence, they nevertheless have no emotional investment in its truth. The point is that intellectual incompetence and desire for a belief to be true are not the only possible

[6] Waugh, *Brideshead Revisited*, p. 738.

causes of a subject's failure. A subject's error might be what cognitive psychologists call 'cold'—the less influenced by affect or emotion, the cooler a cognition is[7]—and yet not be caused by lack of intellectual skill, for it could be that the subject is in general capable of the reasoning required but merely happens to fail in this particular case. The thesis of the cognitive psychologists is that there are certain inferential strategies which, though generally valid, sometimes give the wrong answer. An example of such a strategy is attaching too much weight to evidence which is salient. The less vivid or salient the evidence—the less accessible, concrete, anecdotal, and so on—the more we tend to ignore it, and that makes us susceptible to error. Another example is that, understanding confirmation more easily than disconfirmation, we tend to weight confirming and discrediting evidence differently, and that disposes us to an unwarranted confidence in our beliefs.[8]

So it does not follow that a belief is motivated just because it is false. Indeed, not even the fact that a belief is useful is an infallible indicator that it is motivated. One reason for this is that its convenience might be a coincidence. That something has a beneficial effect cannot on its own explain it. The familiar example is that of the sounds made by the heart which facilitate the diagnosis of heart disease; the fact that they facilitate the diagnosis provides no explanation of why the heart makes these sounds. It is possible that the cold errors mentioned above have a useful effect. Indeed, Nisbett and Ross hint at this, saying,

The social benefits of individually erroneous subjective probabilities may be great even when the individuals pay a high price for the error. We probably would have few novelists, actors or scientists if all potential aspirants to these careers took action based on a normatively justifiable probability of success. We might also have few new products, new medical procedures, new political movements, or new scientific theories.[9]

But since Nisbett and Ross do not suggest that the errors are *explained* by their effects, the idea must be that it is lucky for us

---

[7] For these distinctions, see Pears, *Motivated Irrationality*, pp. 8–9.
[8] See Nisbett and Ross, *Human Inference, passim.*
[9] Ibid. 271.

that people overestimate their chances of success, the over-estimation, happily, being just what is required for the beneficial effects.

Even a rationalization of behaviour need not be motivated. We immediately tend to think of rationalization as a motivated phenomenon, but it is actually quite possible that the belief be only fortuitously agreeable. In his book, *Motivated Irrationality*, David Pears gives an example of a woman who attributes a belief to herself, a false belief which rationalizes her behaviour, although the rationalization is not informed by any motive. This woman has a lot of evidence that her lover is unfaithful but does not believe it, not because she does not want to believe it, but because she makes the cold error of falsely inferring from her behaviour, from the fact that she is continuing the relationship, that she must believe he is faithful. In fact, at an earlier time the woman continued the relationship believing her lover was unfaithful. But subsequently she rationalizes her irrational behaviour by mistakenly inferring from it that at the earlier time she believed he was faithful. This mistake about her past belief is a rationalization because it is an attempt, made after the action, to make sense of it. The false belief is one that, had she had it at the time, would have made her behaviour rational. At the same time, it is not a motivated rationalization because this woman *always* mistakenly attributes rationality where there is none, not only in her own case, but also when she attempts to account for other people's behaviour.[10] Even if we add that she also has the desire not to be irrational, the fit of the belief to the desire would still be luck, if the cause of her rationalization were not the desire, but rather her impartial tendency always to attribute rationality.

A second reason why we are not entitled to conclude that the beliefs of the ruling class are motivated from the fact that they are self-advantaging is that even if their holding them is no coincidence, even if the convenience of the beliefs is a factor in explaining why they are held, it could be the case that the subjects are merely programmed to have the belief which carries survival value, so that there would be no need to

---

[10] Pears, *Motivated Irrationality*, pp. 46–9.

explain it by postulating the action of the will. It does not follow from the fact that you believe that *p* because it serves your interests, that you believe it because you believe it serves your interests. Animals have certain beliefs about their environment, beliefs to which there is survival value attached, and the having of which is therefore in their interests. They believe, for instance, that objects endure, that some are threatening, and so on. We can see how these beliefs are in an animal's interests without having to postulate that it has a conception of itself as a creature with a desire to survive and an interest in holding beliefs which are likely to promote that. To have the beliefs it need not perceive them as in its interests, though it has them because they are in its interests. After all, animals which did not have them would not survive. In the programmed case *a* believes that *p* because it is in *a*'s interests to believe that *p*. In the motivated case *a* believes that *p* because *a believes that it is in a's interests* to believe that *p*. Incidentally, in the programmed case the fact that the belief that *p* serves *a*'s interests is a fact of efficient causation; but in the motivated case what there is is not a fact of causation but a belief about it, namely *a*'s belief that the belief that *p* will serve *a*'s interests. It follows that in the programmed case it *is* in your interests to have the belief; in the motivated case it need not be—not, at any rate, if your belief about what is in your interests is false.

There is also a third reason why the useful beliefs of the bourgeoisie need not be motivated, and that is that even if their explanation does involve a mental mechanism, it need not appeal to anything purposive like a motive or a plan. When there is a motive or a plan there is thought involved, though not necessarily conscious thought. Indeed, it is possible that the thought is necessarily unconscious when there is a motive to believe at work. But there is no reason why, if there is a mental cause for the belief, a motive must be at work. A desire might cause the belief automatically without anything purposive having to intervene. You could play with words here and say that in such a case, too, the result is achieved unconsciously, but it is important to see that 'unconscious' in this sense, of being automatic, or not-thought-out, is not the same 'unconscious' which I used a few sentences back to

qualify the notion of a plan or thought. There unconscious-
ness and purposiveness joined forces; but here, where desire
causes belief automatically, purposiveness is ruled out. I shall
say something later about how it is that desires might affect
beliefs in this way.

3. HAPPY ACCIDENTS AND SYSTEMATIC CORRELATIONS

I said that I would argue that the coherence of the idea of false
consciousness depends on supposing that the rationalizations
of the ruling class are motivated, so I must exclude the other
possibilities I have mentioned. That will be the task of this and
the next two sections.

The first of them, the possibility that the convenience of the
beliefs is merely coincidental, is not a real competitor at all,
being incompatible with that feature of the Marxist account
discussed in the last chapter, namely its materialist claim that
the ideological beliefs of the ruling class are *determined* by their
economic position. I have already explained, in Ch. I. 5, what I
think this means. It means that the beliefs are explained by
their tendency to confer economic benefits. But I also said
there that it could not be a brute fact that something's con-
ferring some benefit should explain its occurrence: such an
explanation can only be legitimate if there exists some underlying causal account of *how* the fact that the item confers
benefits explains its occurrence. Otherwise its role would be
magical.

If we consider analogous explanations in biology for the
moment, the significance of the underlying account will
become clearer. Biologists are entitled to say that the acquisition of organs is explained by the benefits they bring only
because there exists some ordinarily causal account of how
the fact that some organ would benefit a species explains its
acquisition. Of course, there can be disagreement as to what
the correct account is. If we suppose that the useful item
whose acquisition we want to explain is the kidney, then one
explanation is, very briefly, as follows: some members of the
species had kidneys and some did not; because of the nature

of the environment, organisms with kidneys had a greater chance of surviving long enough to reproduce than those that did not; since having a kidney is heritable, over time there came to be many more members of the species with kidneys than without them; and that is how the fact that they have them is explained by the advantages of having them. The mechanism is the Darwinian one of random mutation and differential survival rates. It is worth emphasizing two things about this account. The first is that the occurrence of the first kidney is not explained by its advantages, since mutations do not arise in response to an organism's needs, but satisfy them, when they do, by luck. The second is, as I said earlier, that the occurrence of kidneys is explained by this mechanism even if kidneys are no longer of advantage. The Darwinian account is orthodox, but everyone will know that there are other, rival, accounts of why the consequence explanation holds. Lamarck, for instance, supposed that adaptations which appear in the parents during their own lifetimes as a response to environmental influences are somehow imprinted genetically and thereby transmitted to their offspring. And some people subscribe to a theological explanation, which ascribes the acquisition of the kidney to God's conscious design. In other words, God saw the usefulness of the kidney and supplied it.

Elster argues against Marxism that it is not entitled to claim that social phenomena are explained by their tendency to confer economic benefits, because in the absence of empirical evidence of the mechanism in virtue of which the tendency to have the effects explains the useful items, there is no way in which we can know that the benefits are not coincidental, and there is therefore no possibility of affirming that they *are* explained by their benefits.[11] In large part his animus here seems to be inspired by a fear of opening the door to phoney explanations. Certainly there is a Panglossist tendency, in functionalist sociology especially, to think that to display the beneficial effects of an institution is thereby to explain its existence. But Cohen points out that Marxist social scientists might be in a position to do more than merely point to the benefits conferred by certain isolated superstructural

---

[11] Elster, 'Cohen on Marx's Theory of History', pp. 126–7.

elements. Suppose, for instance, that they can point to a whole range of instances in which, whenever and only when there is a need for beliefs of a certain kind, beliefs of that kind occur. In those circumstances they would be entitled to assert that the occurrence of the beliefs is no coincidence, even if they could not show how the fact that they are advantageous explains their occurrence.[12] In other words, there can be evidence that there is an underlying explanation even if no account can be given of what it is. Sometimes we are inclined to say, 'If there is no explanation of this phenomenon, it is a miracle', and it is legitimate to infer from that that an explanation must exist. So if ruling-class beliefs slot in with ruling-class interests so exactly and so frequently that, if it were a matter of chance it would be miraculous, it is reasonable to infer that the beliefs are explained by their fit with the interests.

We know that Marxism claims that the usefulness of the beliefs of members of the ruling class is no accident, and I have suggested that even in the absence of knowledge of how their usefulness explains them, it could be entitled to make that claim. Obviously a philosophical account would never adduce the empirical evidence which would show that there *is* a systematic tendency to believe in the legitimacy of the system on the part of those who benefit from it, and in what follows I must simply assume that Marx was right about that. But it is not a large assumption. It is highly implausible to suppose that there is absolutely no tendency for members of the ruling-class to hold beliefs which benefit them. In any event, on the assumption that ruling-class beliefs are explained by their fit with ruling-class interests, I shall ask in what follows how it is that their effect might explain them. The aim will be to discover if there is any supporting account Marxism must provide of how the tendency of the beliefs to confer benefits explains them. I have already mentioned the possible candidates for the underlying accounts, the prima-facie possible theories of how the advantages of the beliefs might explain them, but it will be best to begin here by rehearsing them.

---

[12] Cohen, 'Functional Explanation: Reply to Elster', pp. 131–2.

On the first theory, the fact that the subjects hold the beliefs is explained just by the fact that they have the advantages they do. The clearest case of this would be a belief which is genetically imprinted, but there might be other cases which fit the specification too. We are looking for a genetic programme or some other non-mental or non-rational cause.

On the second theory, there is a mental although not an intentional contribution. For an example of this sort of input, think of how I adjust my clothing in response to the weather and change my posture as I feel strained. These actions are to be explained by their advantages to me, but there need be no belief of mine at work; the desire to avoid discomfort affects my actions quite directly. It is not so much that the process is too simple to involve a plan, as that it is a piece of automatic behaviour: I do not think it out. If the ideological case is like this case, where I adjust my clothing as the weather changes, then the happy beliefs will be generated directly by a desire without any intention on the part of the subjects to make themselves accept them.

On the third theory, by contrast, the chain of causation is much less subliminal. The fact that the subjects accept the useful beliefs is explained by the fact that they recognize they have the advantages they do. In other words, their beliefs are motivated. Usually one would have to say 'because they think they have advantages', rather than 'because they recognize they have advantages', there being no general guarantee that behaviour does further the end it is intended to. After all, your behaviour can still be purposive even if you have false beliefs about the situation or the best way to achieve your purpose in that situation. For instance, your behaviour is appropriate to your goal of catching the bus if you cross the road believing that is where the bus stop is. It does not make your behaviour any the less purposive if your belief is false.

In the ideological case, however, there is no need for an operator which does not have implications of success, like 'think', and it is right to say that on the third theory the person who accepts the beliefs recognizes they have the advantages they do. That is because ideological beliefs are said by Marxism *really* to be useful and the third theory has to be compatible with that commitment. So if the best account of the beliefs is that they are motivated, the belief about their advantages will have to be true. We can therefore say that if the beliefs of the ruling class are motivated, then the fact that the subjects accept them will be explained by the fact that they see they are useful, and do whatever they can to preserve or acquire them.

Of course, if it is not simply a matter of their believing something because it is convenient, but rather a matter of their believing it because they see it is convenient, one thing that will need explaining is how the will might come to make such a contribution. I say something about how it can play such a role in Ch. II. 6, where I explain how motivated belief is possible; but first I shall argue that a Marxist is bound to think it must. I shall say more about each of the three models I have described and argue that Marxism is committed to the third. The other two possibilities, the non-rational one, and the one which bypasses purpose, though not explicity ruled out by Marxism are, I shall argue, phantoms.

4. NON-RATIONAL CAUSATION

Consider first the hypothesis that the rationalizations of the ruling class are directly coded for in the genes. No doubt that is true of some useful beliefs. It seems that some beliefs about objects, for instance, are innate. Apparently an infant of two weeks old fears an approaching object and expects it to have tactile qualities. But it would be extremely unlikely that the sorts of belief we are interested in, the illusions of the ruling class about itself, would turn out to be 'wired in'. If ideologies were innate, a member of one class could not adopt a baby born to a member of another, for fear it would turn out hostile.

But perhaps I have been too hasty, having construed too simplistically the way in which a genetic programme could figure in the formation of a belief. Perhaps what is imprinted is not a particular ideology but rather a disposition on the part of those who benefit from a social system to feel justified in taking a larger share, so that what is innate in us is that, placed in a particular kind of social situation, we form a certain kind of belief. Systems of social organization in animals might be pointed to in support of this. Competitive encounters among monkeys, for instance, lead to systems of dominance and submission. Apparently once the systems are established, the maintenance of a dominant position in the hierarchy has nothing to do with continued aggression. It seems rather that both dominant and submissive members recognize that dominant members have first access to mates, food, territory, and so on. It is argued that such hierarchies have benefits, for once the order is stable, aggression and injuries are minimized. Clearly, the ability to slot into the rank is innate. So it is natural to speculate that a hierarchical mentality could have survival value for humans, and be innate in us too, and that such a mentality underlies ideological ways of thought.

But I have two difficulties with that speculation. The first is that there is an obvious difference between the way in which an animal slots into a hierarchy and the way in which people defend their position in a social system. The animal's displays, being 'wired in', are both crude and inflexible. But people who reason ideologically reason in a highly theoretical and subtle way. They are disposed to produce arguments and resist counter-examples. Their ideological constructs are finely tuned, sensitive to changing circumstances, and often novel. I shall be returning to these features of ideological thought when I talk about the need to postulate a strategy; for the moment I only want to make the point that they do not suit the innateness hypothesis.

That is my first difficulty with it. I want to reserve the second but before I say why, it will help to explain the structure of my argument. I am trying to show that the mechanism for ideological belief formation must go through the mind. The innateness hypothesis denies that, but I have given a reason for denying the innateness hypothesis. But even if I am right, and the innateness hypothesis is incorrect, it does not follow straightaway that the mechanism must be mental. If the mechanism were mental, it would be mental phenomena with propositional content, attitudes directed on to propositions, that were involved. To have a belief, for instance, is to have a certain attitude to a proposition—it is to hold the proposition to be true. And to have a desire is to want some proposition to

be true. To be in this area is to be in the area of the rational; it
is also to be in the area of the irrational. Davidson makes this
point. He says: 'irrationality appears only when rationality is
evidently appropriate: where both cause and effect have
contents that have the sort of logical relations that make for
reason or its failure.'[13] In both rational and irrational processes, both cause and effect are states or events with a propositional content. If the states or events with propositional
content which are related as cause and effect are also
rationally related to each other, then the process is rational; if
they do not bear a rational relation to each other, then the
process is irrational. For an example of the former, think of a
belief backing up other beliefs. For an example of the latter,
think of a desire causing a belief.[14] To hypothesize that ideological thought is innate is to hypothesize that we are not in
this area, of the rational and the irrational, at all. It is to locate
the cause of ideological beliefs in the area of the non-rational.
For if the innateness hypothesis is correct, then the beliefs are
neither supported by further beliefs nor even caused by
another state with propositional content, like a desire. The
possibilities can be represented as in Table 2.1.

TABLE 2.1

	The cause of the belief is rationally related to its effect	The cause of the belief is not rationally related to its effect
The cause of the belief can be described in mental terms	I Rational causation	II Irrational causation
The cause of the belief cannot be described in mental terms		III Non-rational causation

[13] Davidson, 'Paradoxes of Irrationality', p. 299.
[14] Ibid. 298.

The innateness hypothesis opts for non-rational causation but it is not the only hypothesis whose effect is to place the cause in the third box. There are other possible hypotheses, one of which I shall describe shortly, whose effect is the same. But the important point for the moment is that to argue for a mental cause of ideological belief, it is not enough to argue against innateness. A more general argument against the possibility of non-rational causation is necessary. In fact, the existence of this more general argument is what I had in mind when I said that there was a second difficulty with the innateness hypothesis, and now it will be seen why I wanted to reserve it: if correct, it disposes not only of the innateness hypothesis but, more generally, of any theory on which there is no mental cause at work. My method will be to describe such a theory, isolate those of its features which rule out a mental cause, and say why they cannot obtain in the ideological case.

Here, then, is an account of how people come to have the advantageous beliefs they do which rejects innateness but still attempts to make do with blind forces. It relies on something like natural selection, but without the genes. This is its proponent speaking: 'I agree with you that the rationalizations of the ruling class would not be provided for by a genetic programme. But there might be some other blind mechanism accounting for how they come to have the congenial beliefs they do. It might be the case that such beliefs are generated in a way which is unrelated to their advantages. Suppose that that is so, and there are all sorts of ideas in circulation, competing for the status of orthodoxy. Now some of those beliefs will be suited to their environment in the sense that they will give people who hold them a better chance of exploiting the available economic resources. And some of them will not be. If Weber is right, a good example is the way in which Calvinism locked in with capitalism. Weber thought that the success of what he called the "rationalist" spirit was nourished by Calvinism's innovatory notion that the pursuit of wealth is, so far from being a vice, a duty. It is obvious how such a belief might legitimate some economic activities, and equally obvious how its medieval predecessor, the notion that you must be wicked if you were poor yesterday but rich today, would subvert them. Now the people who hold the beliefs that are well suited to the economic environment will come, through being in the best position to exploit the resources, to control the society. And of course that explains how those beliefs, though they are not inherited, do get propagated. For the people who hold them, being in control, will also be in a position to influence what information gets communicated. It will be the natural thing for their beliefs to spread by dissemination, contagion even, and that is culture. Nothing mental need be involved in all this. Useful beliefs, beliefs which legitimate an economic set-up and keep it going, will tend to flourish, while heretical beliefs, those that would undermine it, will fail to take root.'

There are two features of this model which are essential to it in so far as it purports to provide a blind mechanism. One is that the belief must drop into people's minds in rather the way that the first kidney occurred. There can be no explanation of its origin or, more exactly, no functional relationship between what caused it and its character. It must be accidental that the belief turns out to satisfy a need. The second feature is that although there is an explanation of the success of the belief, of its persistence, the explanation must bypass the mind. This is really an extra requirement. After all, it is quite possible that a belief should arise by accident but become dominant because people notice how effectively it serves their interests. But a belief which succeeds for that reason is now motivated. What the non-rational model needs, by contrast, is a belief which prevails simply because of the survival value it affords a class in its competition with other classes, and not because the members of that class desire that it be true. It needs a belief which is like the useful belief of an animal, explained merely by the fact that it promotes the animal's interests, not by the fact that it is believed to do that.

But could the sort of belief we are interested in, an inaccurate belief about your motives, be like the useful belief of an animal? Could it be a belief that you just get stuck with, acquiring it by a stroke of luck and automatically prospering by it, so that what you want has nothing to do with the explanation of its acquisition and persistence? Could such a belief, in other words, be in your interests but not desired, which is what the non-rational model implies? There is in general nothing wrong with the assertion that interests are independent of desires. Indeed a Marxist is committed to it, or so I argue in the next chapter. However, I want to show now that there is no sense to the supposition that a flattering belief about your motives, in particular, might serve your interests but satisfy no desire. A misleading picture of your motives can only be in your interests if you desire what it affords you or take an interest in what it caters to: the gap which usually exists between what is in your interests and what you want is here closed off.

Perhaps the best way to see this is to ask how interests are served by the false picture or why any screening of ruling-class motives is necessary. Marxism says that the picture helps to stabilize the society in which the ruling class has a stake: it is said to be essential to the smooth operation of the economic arrangements that the agents who are their beneficiaries should not acknowledge the unpleasing character of their motives. So the illusions of the ruling class secure the existence of the society by making unpalatable activities palatable to those who benefit from them. But the obvious question to ask is why the beneficiaries should need to think of their activities as legitimate. It is easy enough to see why the stability of society depends on the activities of the ruling class seeming legitimate in the eyes of the subordinate class. But why need the rulers be deceived as well? Would not it be enough for them to convince the ruled, by propaganda perhaps, or manipulation? The point here is that the fact that the beneficiaries need to believe in the respectability of their motives calls for explanation. Why would they do less well for themselves if they did not have that belief? I suggest that the question can only be answered on the assumption that people like to think well of themselves. It can only be because they *desire* to see their actions and motivations as unexploitative that, if they saw them as exploitative, they would be less inclined to pursue their economic activities and so do less well for themselves. If it were not important to them if they thought badly of themselves, their ignorance of their real motives would do them no good. It would cater to no interest. So their picture of their motives must be caused by the fact that their motives matter to them. But of course their motives' mattering to them is something psychological. So a mental state is playing an essential part in the explanation of why the beliefs are held. The upshot is that the Marxist thesis that the members of the ruling class need to be ignorant of their motives, if the society in which they have a stake is to run smoothly, only makes sense on an assumption about the way in which we like to represent ourselves to ourselves.

A way to bring out the dependence of the need on a desire here is to look at some examples where there is no such dependence. There are the genetically programmed beliefs of animals, of course, which I mentioned before; but it is inter-esting that there are cases of belief which are somewhat more like ideological belief although, as with the animals' beliefs, there is no desire in operation. Pears argues, for instance that it is plausible to think that sometimes when our thinking is coloured by emotions like fear and jealousy, there is no desire at work, nature simply having programmed us to think in a certain way. Consider fear. When we are caused to exaggerate danger by fear, the exaggeration benefits us for it makes sure that we avoid the danger. But there is no *desire* to form the exaggerated belief and no plan. There may be a desire for the ulterior goal, which is safety, but because the belief is not seen as a means to the ulterior goal there is no desire to form it—indeed it is an intrinsically unpleasant belief—and so the emotive thinking which achieves the ulterior goal must be somehow programmed.[15] The contrast with the ideological case is obvious. In the fear case the exaggeration of the danger is explained just by the need the exaggeration serves. Desire, even desire for the ulterior goal of safety, plays no explanatory role in the belief's occurrence. But in the ideological case there is neither a need nor a harm if there is not a desire. It is because people desire to think well of themselves that they need to be ignorant of how single-minded is their pursuit of their economic interests. So a desire plays an essential role in explaining why the belief is held.

It is also interesting that it is only where you are benefited by your own misperceptions that you must have the desire to think well of yourself. For you can be benefited by someone

---

[15] Pears, *Motivated Irrationality*, pp. 42–4.

else's over-generous interpretation of your motives without having that desire. Suppose, for instance, that a man treats the woman he is involved with very shabbily, but she persists in interpreting his actions in the most charitable light. Suppose also that this irritates him; he wants her to leave him alone and he wishes that she would perceive his character more accurately. It can still be the case that he is benefited by her indulgent beliefs. Perhaps his shabby behaviour and his irritation are self-destructive and the continued affair is really in his interests. Here the woman's beliefs satisfy a need but no desire of his. But now suppose it is the *man* who interprets his actions over-charitably. There is a big difference if the benefits accrue from *self*-indulgence. Any story we tell about how his own indulgent interpretations benefit him, or what the harm would be if he saw things straight, has to assume that he does not want to be someone who treats others badly. Perhaps he would end the relationship which benefited him if he saw his behaviour for what it was. But he would only do that if he did not want to be the sort of person who acts in a shabby way. Perhaps he would become depressed if he saw his actions in their true light, whereas the false picture keeps him buoyant. But if he did not care about how he dealt with the woman, there would be no danger of depression. He can only benefit from his false picture, and suffer a corresponding harm from the true one, if he desires to be a certain kind of person. Without the desire there is no point to the misperception. The more general point here is that beliefs which cater to vanities cannot be in our interests, cannot make things go well for us, unless we care about our self-image. And of course the ideological beliefs which are the subject of this discussion are just such beliefs, catering as they do to a vanity about character.

I have argued that when the bourgeoisie misperceive their motives, that can only serve their interests if they desire to think well of themselves. But someone might object to this claim as follows: 'Suppose a politician who has been accused of corruption is required to defend herself. She happens to believe her actions are justified and the belief benefits her because it has the effect of making her more convincing in her defence. However, she also happens not to care whether her actions are justified or not. Isn't this a case of someone who is

benefited by misconstruing her actions although she has no
desire to think well of herself?' This might seem an especially
compelling objection in that Marx himself sometimes talks as
if the reason that members of the ruling class need to be
wrong about their motives is that, if they are not wrong, they
will be less good at convincing others that they have a right to
be in power. There is, for instance, the passage in *The German
Ideology* which I quoted in the Introduction, which suggests
that the success of the ruling class depends on its members
perceiving and presenting their interests as non-sectional. But
in fact, this is no real objection. For one thing, the politician
example is not analogous to the ideological case. For the fact
that the politician is benefited by her belief does not explain
her holding the belief. How could it? It is coincidence that she
happens to hold the belief which enables her to be convincing.
But *ex hypothesi* it is not just luck that the flattering beliefs of
members of the ruling class are well suited to their interests.
Secondly, the phenomenon described by the objector could
never happen generally. It would be miraculous if a whole
class of people came to their convenient beliefs in this
accidental way. Thirdly, it is not even clear that what is
described in the case of the politician really makes sense. For
why should someone who genuinely believes her actions are
justified be better at persuading others than someone who
merely pretends to believe that? Why are we unsuccessful at
deceiving others? The only possible answer to this question is:
because we *care* about how our actions appear to ourselves
and so, if we feel worried on that count, our unease com-
municates itself. Likewise, if it is true that the workers are
more likely to be convinced by a story which is genuinely
believed rather than just contrived or fabricated by the
bourgeoisie, that could only be because the bourgeoisie are
concerned about their self-image. It could only be because
they care about how their actions appear to themselves that
they feel uneasy and are bad at deceiving others.

It is worth mentioning that there is a nice fit here between
Marxism and some discoveries of social psychology. For one
thing, psychologists have found that we like to think we live in
a just world and are often convinced that our victims deserve

their fate.[16] And the fact that we tend to believe we live in a world in which our victims get what they deserve is obvious support for the Marxist claim that people tend to glamorize their motives and put themselves in the clear. But an even more interesting psychological finding is that the tendency to derogate victims is a rationalization for behaviour which is dissonant with beliefs. The general idea is that human beings are motivated to reduce dissonance, dissonance being a discrepancy between beliefs or between behaviour and beliefs. The cognition, 'I smoke cigarettes', for instance, is dissonant with the cognition, 'cigarette smoking causes disease'. One way to eliminate the dissonance is to give up smoking. If you fail at that, consistency theories predict that you will be likely to attempt an adjustment to the other cognition, perhaps by minimizing the threat.[17] Now psychologists have found that the reason we think that the victims of our injustice deserve their fate is because that is a way to reduce the dissonance we experience between how we behave and our high-minded images of ourselves.[18] In other words, the desire to think well of ourselves explains our view of a just world.

This shows that Elster is wrong to claim, as he does, that the Marxist theory of ideology would do better to look for a foothold in social–psychological theories rather than in what he calls 'structural and functionalist' theories, implying that these are rivals. In *Sour Grapes* he says, 'Against the structural and the functionalist approaches I would like to insist on the need for an understanding of the psychological mechanisms by which ideological beliefs are formed and entrenched.'[19] But I think that what I have said shows that there is no real conflict of approaches here. I have argued that what Elster calls a functionalist approach to ideology (ideological rationalizations serve a purpose and are explained by it) must be prepared to postulate a desire to preserve a certain idea of the self. And in the preceding paragraph I said that social psychology suggests that such a desire does lie behind a

[16] Lerner, 'The desire for justice and reactions to victims', p. 207.
[17] Aronson, *The Social Animal*, p. 89.
[18] Ibid. 120–6.
[19] Elster, *Sour Grapes*, p. 142.

comforting view of the world. So social psychology provides evidence for the truth of a claim to which the 'functionalist' approach is committed.

But perhaps there is another kind of rivalry. I have argued in this section that the inaccurate but useful picture of their motives held by the bourgeoisie must be powered by a desire, the desire to respect themselves. But it might be wondered whether the essential role played by this psychological element in the Marxist account is compatible with other aspects of Marx's thought and, in particular, with his distinctive brand of determinism. It might be said that if Marxism *is* committed to some mental input to explain how it is that ideological rationalizations are explained by their advantages, that is bad news for Marxism. For Marxism is equally, and centrally, committed to the claim that 'Men make their own history, but they do not make it just as they please';[20] that 'men enter into definite relations that are indispensable and independent of their will, relations of production ... on which rise a legal and political superstructure'.[21] Honderich argues something like this when he says it is illicit for a Marxist to appeal to agents' beliefs and desires in an account of why Marx's consequence explanations are true, for such an appeal is incompatible with Marx's view about the irrelevance to history of our 'will' and 'consciousness'.[22]

But I do not think the objection succeeds. I have said that the only reason ideological rationalizations could be required for the stability of the economic structure, as they are said by Marx to be, is because people feel uncomfortable when they profit from exploitation, and the most natural interpretation of what Marx meant by the irrelevance of our will and consciousness to history does not threaten that claim. I think that Marx meant that our will is irrelevant in the sense that our beliefs and desires are outside our control, being determined by the economic features of our society. But this certainly does not imply that historical developments occur *independently* of what we want and believe, or that our beliefs and desires play no role in historical events. For the route

---

[20] *The Eighteenth Brumaire of Louis Bonaparte*, p. 103.

[21] Preface to *A Contribution to the Critique of Political Economy*, pp. 182–3.

[22] Honderich, 'Against Teleological Historical Materialism', pp. 465, 467.

from economic conditions to historical outcomes might involve men and women acting in certain ways on the basis of their admittedly determined beliefs and desires. When Marx says that individuals 'are dealt with only in so far as they are the personifications of economic categories, embodiments of particular class-relations and class interests',[23] this implies that what people want is dictated by their position in the economic structure, not that their desires play no role in history. So there is, after all, room for a fact about people's psychology to explain why rationalizations should have the stabilizing effect on society they do.

5. DESIRES AND PLANS

We know that Marx says that the misperceptions of the bourgeoisie are explained by the interests they serve. But how do their advantages explain them? In the last section I argued against any theory according to which the causation of the rationalizations is non-rational, that is, on which the cause cannot be identified under a mental description. I argued that if the cause were not identifiable as mental, it would have to be true of the rationalizations not only that they are random—the explanation of their origin having nothing to do with their usefulness—but also that the explanation of their success bypasses the mind. I argued, however, that it is impossible for them to have those features, for the interest which the false beliefs serve depends on the subjects' having a certain kind of desire. In a nutshell: if their desires did not play a role here it is not clear why any screening of their motives would be necessary at all. Consequently ideological beliefs about motives cannot be explained just by the fact that they serve interests; some reference has also to be made to a desire. But then what explains them is something mental.

But nothing I have said so far proves that anything so strong as the purposive promotion of belief is involved. For it is not the case that there are only two possibilities here—either non-mental causation of ideological rationalizations or self-induced belief. There is an intermediate possibility, which is

---

[23] Preface to first German edn. of *Capital*, i. 20–1.

that ideological beliefs might be automatically caused by
desire. After all, it seems that *actions* can be automatically
affected by desire. Just as lizards are disposed to change their
angle to the sun, I am disposed to adjust my clothes, holding
my coat more firmly around me when the wind blows, or
easing my collar away from my neck when I feel clammy, on
cues from the environment perceived subliminally. My action
caters to the desire to keep comfortably warm, but at the same
time there need be no thought involved. It can happen automatically. And it is legitimate to wonder whether, if actions
can respond in this way to desire, *beliefs* might not respond
analogously. Perhaps the desire to preserve an appropriate
self-image, which I have argued is implicated in the causation
of ideological rationalizations, directly or automatically produces them without the intervention of the will. Perhaps what
happens is that, receiving discomfort signals from evidence for
the fact that they benefit from exploitative economic arrangements, the members of the ruling class react mechanically so
as to restore the balance. Perhaps it is a reflex to get bored
with the topic, or to turn their attention to something else.
Here a desire would be involved, namely a desire that certain
unpleasant facts about themselves should not be true, but
since there is nothing purposive in it, the will would be short-
circuited.

In one sense of the term, the process I have described is
unconscious but in another sense it need not be. It is unconscious in the sense that it does not involve deliberation, but it
is not necessarily unconscious in the sense that it is a process
of which we must be unaware. It is in general possible to
observe our reflex behaviour and I think it is even possible to
be aware of the reflex effects of desire on our beliefs, although
this is slightly more problematic because of the element of
irrationality involved in recognizing that a desire has caused a
belief, a desire to believe p not being a reason to believe p.[24]
Nevertheless Pears has shown that if your irrationality does

---

[24] Davidson points out that it is not irrational in itself to believe something
because you wish it were true, because 'we are not in general responsible for the
causes of our thoughts'. It only becomes irrational when you know why you have
the belief and that you would not have it were it not for the wish. See 'Deception
and Division', pp. 142–3.

not involve you in an outright contradiction, the operation of a desire is not automatically blocked by consciousness of its workings. This is easiest to see in mild cases of irrationality, where a belief for which there is no supporting evidence, or for which there is equal evidence, both for and against, is formed under the influence of a desire. But even where the weight of inductive evidence is against a belief, it is still possible for a person to persist in the belief and know that the cause of the persistence is the influence of a desire. The reason is that inductive evidence 'allows people the latitude to refuse to make their beliefs conform to it even though they are perfectly aware of what they are doing'.[25] Indeed, Pears argues that you can even consciously believe contradictory propositions, provided that the two beliefs are compartmentalized or remain at a distance from each other in your mind, perhaps because they are associated with different roles you play.[26] An extreme example of this might be multiple personality. Naturally it will be a difficult achievement to maintain an irrational belief in the circumstances described, just because a desire is not the right kind of cause for a belief. But at most that suggests that it is unlikely, not impossible, that the belief will survive consciousness of its origins.[27]

Someone who conceded the phenomenon of conscious irrational belief might nevertheless insist that it must involve at least some idiosyncrasy on the part of the subject and the propulsive contribution of a desire, that the rational belief that is rejected must always involve some painful fact and the belief actually formed always bring satisfaction. But even that is not true, or so I argue in Chapter V. There I discuss beliefs which are insulated from the operation of the intellect although the causal role is not played by desire. The beliefs are instead a natural response to very vivid but unreliable experiential evidence. However, what is true is that where the well-founded belief is painful, the phenomenon is more familiar. For instance, everyone will know how easy it is to exploit the fact that inductive evidence never guarantees that a proposition is true, to judge that there is no need to stop a

[25] Pears, *Motivated Irrationality*, pp. 75–6.
[26] Ibid. 76.
[27] Ibid. 77–8.

bad habit, like smoking or drinking, or to start a good one, like taking exercise.

What is more, the process is greatly facilitated when the desired belief is a belief in which a *group* of people take an interest. It seems to be an unhappy fact about us that we are much less concerned about the causes of our beliefs when we hold them in common with other members of a group to which we belong. Think of something like house spirit at school. Children are not led by evidence to believe their house is best, but that their house is best is a belief which gives satisfaction to all the children in the house. They fairly easily form the belief which gives satisfaction to all and know that that is why they are led to it, and the reason seems to be that all they are called on to do is to acquiesce in a belief which is already held by others with whom they have interests in common. There is much less which has to happen here, where the belief is ritualized or institutionalized, than has to happen in the bad habit case, where the belief needs more of a push from the desire.

Another point is that though the phenomenon of consciously believing something against the weight of the evidence occurs relatively familiarly in everyday life, there is an extra ingredient in the group, and especially the political, case which is likely to make it proceed more smoothly, and that is the existence of an established and comprehensive vocabulary which, when people latch on to it, facilitates the formation of belief. Orwell famously talked about this connection between the hypnotizing or numbing use of clichés and political disingenuousness, saying:

In our time, political speech and writing are largely the defence of the indefensible. Things like the continuance of British rule in India, the Russian purges and deportations, the dropping of the atom bombs on Japan, can indeed be defended, but only by arguments which are too brutal for most people to face, and which do not square with the professed aims of political parties. Thus political language has to consist largely of euphemism, question begging and sheer cloudy vagueness. Defenceless villages are bombarded from the air, the inhabitants driven into the countryside, the cattle machine-gunned, the huts set on fire with incendiary bullets: this is called *pacification.* Millions of peasants are robbed of their farms and sent trudging along the roads with no more than they can carry: this is called *transfer of population* or *rectification of frontiers*. People are imprisoned for years without trial, or shot in the back of the neck or sent to die of scurvy in Arctic lumber camps: this is called *elimination of unreliable elements*.[28]

Something similar is the availability of historical myths and legends. People draw on them and they are, as Marx pointed out, a potent stimulus to belief and action: 'In ... periods of revolutionary crisis,' Marx said, '[men] anxiously conjure up the spirits of the past to their service and borrow from them names, battle-cries and costumes in order to present the new scene of world history in this time-honoured disguise and this borrowed language.'[29]

We have seen that it is possible for beliefs directly to respond to desires, and that the process can even happen with full awareness, particularly where it is a matter of holding a belief which benefits one as a member of a group. Now that might seem to account very economically for the phenomenon of false consciousness, but in fact it can be shown that ideological rationalizations cannot be explained by the rudimentary hypothesis that they are automatic responses to disturbing cues. I am going to argue that it has to be more complicated than that and that we have to suppose that there is an intentional element operating.

The first thing to decide is in what circumstances the complication would be required. One difference between automatic behaviour and behaviour which is informed by a purpose or intention seems to lie in this, that purposive behaviour is informed by a thought about the appropriateness of the means chosen to the end aimed at, whereas automatic behaviour involves routine responses to a stimulus. The most obvious cases of the latter are low down on the phylogenetic scale where organisms are entirely stimulus-bound and respond reflexively. The rigid and stereotyped reactions we observe here are due to inherited neural properties, but there is also automatic behaviour which is not innate. There may have been thought at one time in behaviour which is now

---

[28] Orwell, 'Politics and the English Language', p. 366.
[29] *The Eighteenth Brumaire of Louis Bonaparte*, p. 104.

routine. Where automatic behaviour is inflexible, purposive behaviour is adaptable. Braithwaite describes this as its 'plasticity', meaning to capture the way in which a creature aiming at a goal is able to reach it from many different starting points.[30]

'But couldn't we redescribe its behaviour by detailing all the stimuli it has encountered and all the ways it has responded to them, and in that way write out the notion of a purpose?' Well, suppose we did that. We should end up with a disjunction of correlations, $S_1 \rightarrow R_1$, $S_2 \rightarrow R_2$, ... $S_n \rightarrow R_n$. All the disjunction tells us is that the creature responds in this way to this stimulus and in that way to that stimulus. The correlations display no order. But it is a different matter with the description of the creature as doing whatever, in each kind of situation, it thinks would lead to its achieving its purpose. To say what end all the bits of behaviour are thought to secure is to pick out what they have in common: the creature's doing something in one situation and something else in another is its doing whatever in each situation is thought to lead to its achieving its purpose. Clearly, as the number of $S \rightarrow R$ correlations grows, the purposive account increasingly becomes the only way to understand what the creature is doing. For in fixing on the common features, in discerning an order, it gives us a unitary account of the behaviour, in contrast with the disjunction of correlations which gives only a multiple account. So the more complex a creature's behaviour (the higher the value of n), the more we are forced to invoke a purpose if we are to understand what it is up to. We cannot make do without that notion.[31]

I have said that adaptability suggests a purpose at work but there is another indicator of purposive behaviour which I have not yet mentioned, something additional to adaptability. It is the ability to take a previously unheard of step. Of course, human beings are only relatively capable of novel behaviour; there must be some solutions to problems which are outside our repertoire and impossible for us. However, it is no miracle in our case should someone improvise a route to a goal while

---

[30] Braithwaite, *Scientific Explanation*, ch. 10.

[31] This is a version of an argument of Charles Taylor's in *The Explanation of Behaviour* (pp. 13–14). See also Taylor, 'Teleological Explanation', p. 143.

lacking past experience of behaviour of that kind achieving that end; whereas much lower down in the phylogenetic scale, there is literally no possibility of improvisation.

We must now go back to the rationalizations of the ruling class and ask whether they can be handled by the exiguous hypothesis that they are automatic and routine responses to stimuli which threaten to undermine pleasing beliefs about the self, or whether we need the more elaborate hypothesis that there is a strategy operating. It is relevant to this question that it is often said that it is essential to ideological beliefs that they are 'closed'. And what that is meant to point to is the way in which people resist the falsification of their ideologies. Certainly, that may happen with non-ideological beliefs too— for instance, when a scientist is attached to a theory—but exactly the same thing is going on in those cases as always goes on in the ideological case. What gives it away is that the belief is not held in a spirit of enquiry. Consider the subjects who have the wrong view of their motivation. They will have an elaborate story about their motives; they will have made all sorts of *ad hoc* adjustments to the beliefs, rationalizing things which would normally worry them, explaining them away; they will be defensive when challenged, reluctant to look too closely, and so on.

A sceptic might challenge what is implicitly assumed here, namely that a protective attitude towards theories is something suspect. But even if it is true that a certain amount of conservatism is a good thing and that giving the benefit of the doubt to a well-established theory is often rational, that is very different from the kind of digging in that acceptance of an ideology provokes. The charity towards a theory's predictive failures of someone who is not emotionally committed to the theory is always qualified, and such a person remains on the look-out for really hopeless defects. But the defence of ideological beliefs is something different. It is come-what-may.

Now this is all too complex and too versatile for it to be true that the beliefs of the ruling class could be held relatively innocently, as the reflex or automatic outcome of the operation of a desire. We must suppose there is deliberation because the desire produces a variety of means to the end. The subjects behave in a way which is ultra-sensitive to the

changing situations in which their belief may be shown to be
false. Their behaviour is so finely attuned to so many circumstances, so plastic, and also so ingenious, that the only way to
understand it is to impute to them the intention of seeing
themselves in a certain way and all this as action taken to
secure the favoured belief. We have to see them as determined
to hold fast to it no matter what.

Notice that I do not need to say that everyone in the ruling
class has to operate with a strategy. There is room in my
account for what probably does happen, for there being, in the
case of some of its members, capitulation to the desired belief
rather than its intentional production. There is bound to be a
bandwagon effect, some of the prevailing conviction being
explicable simply by the voguishness of it all. Indeed, Marx
and Engels themselves hint at that possibility. In *The German
Ideology* they say:

inside [the ruling] class one part appears as the thinkers of the class
(its active, conceptive ideologists, who make the formation of the
illusions of the class about itself their chief source of livelihood),
while the others' attitude to these ideas and illusions is more passive
and receptive, because they are in reality the active members of this
class and have less time to make up illusions and ideas about themselves.[32]

Of those who are more 'passive and receptive' it could be true,
and probably is, that they merely surrender to belief; but the
thinking of the ideologues is too systematic to be explained
like that. And as long as the theorizing is purposive there is a
need for the kind of account I have given, in terms of motivated belief. Some may passively acquiesce in what was
actively organized by others and those who are 'passive and
receptive' may find a vocabulary and mythology ready to
hand. But the vocabulary had to be coined and the mythology,
as Marx puts it, borrowed.

6. HOW MOTIVATED MISTAKES ARE POSSIBLE

I have argued that the Marxist account only makes sense on
the supposition that members of the ruling class are motivated

---

[32] *The German Ideology*, p. 60.

to see themselves in a certain way. But that is a problematic supposition. For it is one thing to succumb in your beliefs to the influence of a wish; it is another intentionally to act so as to achieve a desired belief. Beliefs are answerable to the way the world is and therefore you cannot just straightforwardly set about believing something,[33] though you may of course easily set about pretending you do. Marxism is, however, clear that the bourgeoisie genuinely believe their motives are respectable. They are not said to be liars or hypocrites. How then are we to understand their achievement? To answer that question will be the task of this section, thus delivering on the promise I gave at the beginning of Ch. II. 2, that I should explain not only why the beliefs of the bourgeoisie must be motivated but also how motivated belief is possible.

A glib reply would be that even if there is no direct road to belief, there is at least the more circuitous route of self-deception. But that is more to restate the problem than to answer it. For, as we shall see, if we take the name 'self-deception' literally, their achievement may seem impossible; on the other hand, if we reform the concept, we run the risk of not doing justice to the distinctiveness of the phenomenon. In fact, both of these approaches are common in the literature and sometimes it is assumed, as Patrick Gardiner points out, that they are the only possibilities.[34] I shall say only a bit about these difficulties, confining myself to what is necessary to show that the concept of false consciousness does not confront insuperable obstacles at this point.

Those who take the name 'self-deception' literally would model the phenomenon on the case of straightforward deception, the deception of one person by another. Since in the 'other-deception' case, the deceiver believes not-p and causes another to believe p, it is thought that if I deceive myself I must believe not-p and cause myself to believe p. It is then tempting to conclude that self-deception is impossible. For, as Sartre argues in *Being and Nothingness*, it is impossible to suppose that someone could simultaneously believe both p

---

[33] Bernard Williams makes this point, that because beliefs aim at truth it is impossible to believe at will, just like that. See 'Deciding to Believe', pp. 147–9.
[34] Gardiner, 'Error, Faith, and Self-Deception', p. 51.

and not-*p*; also, if I lie, then I must be aware of the deception, but if I am aware of the deception it cannot succeed.[35]

Some who take this argument seriously but wish to save self-deception argue for a very different understanding of what self-deception involves. Canfield and Gustafson, for instance, say that what is going on in self-deception is that the subject believes something in 'belief-adverse circumstances', these being circumstances which strongly suggest the opposite conclusion.[36] If you take this at face value, it can make no sense of the distinctiveness of self-deception, of the difference between self-deception and ordinary error. After all, not all people who hold unjustified beliefs are deceiving themselves; the fault may be simple incompetence. It might be true, as Siegler says, that there are many circumstances in which we accuse someone of self-deception. For instance, according to him, 'I have been deceiving myself' can sometimes amount to no more than a way of saying that I ought to have known better.[37] But whatever goes on at the outposts of the concept, it is clear that in the central cases self-deception involves more than mere confusion. On the other hand, if we read an extra ingredient into Canfield and Gustafson's analysis, so as to accommodate that difference, we seem to be led back to Sartre's conclusion. For it might seem that what is distinctive about self-deception is the recognition by the subject of the 'adversity' to belief of the circumstances—but then how are we to explain the acquisition of the belief?[38]

I think Pears is right to say that one of the difficulties in this area is quite superficial. In particular, it is a superficial difficulty that we happen to be saddled with the name 'self-deception', with its troublesome implication that someone believes the conjunction of two contradictory propositions. The solution to that is to see that I can deceive myself that *p* without accepting or ever having accepted the truth of not-*p*. There is no reason that self-deception should be as florid as

[35] Sartre, *Being and Nothingness*, p. 49.

[36] Canfield and Gustafson, 'Self-Deception', p. 35.

[37] Siegler, 'Demos on Lying to Oneself, p. 474.

[38] I have drawn on Gardiner's article ('Error, Faith, and Self-Deception') for the points made in this paragraph and the one preceding it. See pp. 37–43.

the name suggests: I can be deceiving myself even if I am not *literally* deceiving myself.[39]

For instance, I can get myself to believe something through averting my gaze from the truth rather than through actually changing my mind about what is false. Suppose I suspect something is true of myself but would prefer it if that were not so. To preserve the more flattering picture of my character, I avoid the negative evidence and assiduously search out the positive. If anybody suggests that it is really something unlikeable which is motivating me, I become defensive; if the thought occurs to me unprompted I rely on special pleading. I am anxiously protective towards the favoured belief in a myriad ways. But I need not know the belief is false to do all this. It is just that, wanting something to be true, I manœuvre my way round what I suspect, if I looked closely enough, would show it to be false.

The interesting thing about this sort of case is, as Pears points out, that it is hardly paradoxical at all. No conjunction of contradictory propositions is believed; all there is is the co-existence of the belief that p with the suspicion that possibly not-p. The only possible piece of irrationality might be in the subject's failure to acquire all the relevant evidence, but there is at any rate nothing impossible or incoherent in that. For the same reason, there is no incoherence in the subject's plan.[40]

A possible objection to the description of this case is that I must know my belief is false in order successfully to steer my way around the evidence. After all, how do I know where *not* to look? But I do not think the objection succeeds. All I have to know in order to know where not to look is that, if I look there, I might be led to an unwanted belief. I certainly need not know that I will be led to an unwanted belief. Indeed, if I did already know that, there could be no point in failing to collect the evidence.

The more problematic form of self-deception involves the intentional production of a belief not justified by evidence already gathered. Here there is much more to the irrationality

---

[39] Pears, *Motivated Irrationality*, pp. 28–9.
[40] Pears, 'The Paradoxes of Self-Deception', in *Questions in the Philosophy of Mind*, pp. 86–7.

than a mere failure to accumulate all the relevant evidence, and the only way to understand it is to divide the mind and suppose that there is more than one system at work within the person. If, in other words, a desire to believe something takes the form of a complex plan to *manufacture* belief, such a plan must be ascribed to some sub-system within the mind, which deceives the main system, reacting and making adjustments as the main system demands them. Otherwise, as Pears points out, there would be no way to explain how the strategy conforms so accurately and is so sensitive to the changing needs of the self-deceiver.[41]

There is, however, more than one way to effect the division.[42] Freud thought that the main system contains what is conscious and the sub-system what is unconscious. But Davidson divides the mind along different lines, saying that it is 'the breakdown of reason-relations [which] defines the boundary of a sub-division'.[43] In other words, if a mental element fails to interact in its normal rational way with another mental element, causing but not rationalizing it, there is an automatic assignment of those elements to different territories.[44] So the partitioning takes place along functional lines—if a mental element functions improperly, causing another element to which it bears no rational relation, it is automatically segregated from its effect and condemned to a sub-system—and there is no implication that what is in the sub-system is inaccessible to consciousness. At the same time, the functional theory is not incompatible with Freud's theory, that some failure of consciousness explains how the irrationality occurs, and Davidson says that the assumption of unconscious elements can be brought in, to enhance explanatory power, when necessary.[45] Certainly that assumption does

[41] See Pears, *Motivated Irrationality*, pp. 63, 89. Alfred Mele argues that Pears is wrong and that a strategy of manipulating information does not have to be ascribed to a sub-system within the mind. But in the cases he describes a desire motivates the employment of a self-deceptive strategy in the absence of an intention to deceive oneself. And even if that is possible, it does not threaten the point that when the self-deceiver *intends* the deception, the hypothesis of the divided mind is necessary. See Mele, *Irrationality*, pp. 144–9.

[42] Pears, *Motivated Irrationality*, pp. 68–9.

[43] Davidson, 'Paradoxes of Irrationality', p. 304.

[44] Ibid. 298–303.

[45] Ibid. 304–5.

seem necessary, as Pears points out, to handle the paradox of self-deception when it is literally construed. For it is impossible simultaneously to believe two evidently contradictory propositions, so we must postulate some failure of consciousness to explain irrationality that extreme.[46]

All this can be readily applied to the ideological case. First, there is no need for the paradoxical supposition that those who have the flattering view of their motivation also have a true picture of it. If they merely suspect that the flattering view is inaccurate, there is no problematic implication that they are currently 'really' aware of its defects. It is not even implied that at some time in the past they were more self-aware. And if so, what they achieve is far from impossible.

Second, if the desire of the bourgeoisie to think well of themselves takes the form of a plan actually to manufacture belief, then that is a more problematic form of self-deception and the only way to understand it is to suppose that the plan is the plan of a sub-system within the mind. For it cannot be supposed, as I have already said, that an undivided agent could have a technique for producing belief. I have already argued that the Marxist account requires two quite different motives. Now we see that there have to be not only two motives, but also two mistakes. Think of Lady Marchmain's belief that the rich may sin if they covet the privileges of the poor. She redescribes her desire to preserve her privileges (her first motive), converting it into a kind of onerous duty (her first mistake). I argued that the source of such a mistake must lie in a second motive, the desire to think well of herself or *amour-propre*. Lady Marchmain's mistaking her motive for defending her privileges is thus itself motivated: it is motivated by the desire to think well of herself. But if her desire to think well of herself takes the form of a self-deceptive strategy aimed at producing the appropriate belief, the desire must be the desire of an autonomous sub-system within her which wants the main system to form the belief and manipulates it to achieve the desired result. And obviously, if the plan works, the main system will be ignorant of the desire's campaign, which is her second mistake. It is tempting to think that the

<hr>

[46] Pears, *Motivated Irrationality*, p. 76.

mere existence of the motive must be as unavailable to the main system as its operations, that it is a motive which is unavowable by the subject and has to be misconstrued by her. But that would be wrong. It is quite possible that Lady Marchmain should admit that she likes to think well of herself. All that she must deny is that it is the desire to think well of herself which has caused her belief that it is not wrong to 'have so many beautiful things'.[47] So if the irrationality of the bourgeoisie is deep, if they actually intend the deception, there is a second mistake which has to accompany the first one: this second mistake is a mistake about the causal connection between a motive and their mistake about their motives.

*

This chapter has canvassed various possible ways in which the fact that a belief serves class interests could lead to the members of the class having that belief.

One hypothesis was that the belief is genetically programmed, or that at least the disposition to form the belief when placed in a certain kind of social situation is genetically programmed. I argued that this view shares with any view on which the cause of the belief is not a psychological state a fatal defect, namely that there is no independently existing interest for the belief to serve, for there is no interest to which the belief can cater in the absence of a desire on the part of the class members to cultivate an attractive self-image.

A second hypothesis was that such a desire might directly cause the belief. Just as a desire to avoid discomfort can cause action as a reflex response to an uncomfortable situation, could not a desire to think well of yourself cause the appropriate belief as an automatic response to a situation in which your motives are in question? This is a history which makes the reference to psychological states I claimed was essential, but bypasses the will, because the desire produces the belief directly, without the mediating influence of a plan or strategy.

The last hypothesis was that the subjects are motivated by

---

[47] Pears distinguishes lack of awareness of a wish from lack of awareness of its operation in 'Motivated Irrationality, Freudian Theory and Cognitive Dissonance', p. 265.

either the suspicion or the thought that an unwanted belief is true actually to do something: in the one case to avoid acquiring evidence which points in the direction of the unwanted belief suspected to be true, and in the other to produce a belief in its negation, the model in both cases being motivated behaviour. I argued that only this last hypothesis, that there is the intentional deployment of a strategy, whether to maintain or to manufacture belief, accommodates the subtle and elastic nature of ideological thought, the fact that it is finely tuned to many beliefs about circumstances, and its sensitivity to details. I pointed out that there is no need to deny that some members of the class might be passive in respect of their desires. But that could never be the whole story: some members of the class must have the intention to 'make up illusions and ideas about themselves'.

III

Unhappy Desires

1. 'INHUMAN, SOPHISTICATED, UNNATURAL AND IMAGINARY APPETITES'

Not all false consciousness is a matter of members of the ruling class masking or rationalizing their pursuit of economic interests. There is also the false consciousness which consists in the acquiescence of the proletariat in an economic system which oppresses it. It is really later Marxists who have elaborated on this idea, confronted by the anomaly that the working class has turned out to be much more divided and much less radical than Marx predicted. Their response has been to say that workers who lack revolutionary enthusiasm are directed towards the wrong goals in their actions, that they have inauthentic values, or inappropriate desires, or false needs. There are hints of this idea, that an agent's motivations can be faulty, already in Marx, particularly in the *Economic and Philosophic Manuscripts*, where he distinguishes between 'crude' and 'human' needs in the course of an attack on the obsessive consumption which characterizes a system of private property. Under capitalism, says Marx, individuals have 'stupid and one-sided'[1] desires for more and more possessions, and the money required to buy them, so that all passions and all activity come to be 'submerged in avarice'.[2] 'Every new product', he continues,

represents a new *potentiality* of mutual swindling and mutual plundering ... The extension of products and needs becomes a *contriving* and ever-*calculating* subservience to inhuman, sophisticated, unnatural and *imaginary* appetites. Private property does not know how to change crude need into *human* need ... No eunuch flatters his despot more basely or uses more despicable means to stimulate his dulled capacity for pleasure than does the industrial eunuch—the

[1] *Economic and Philosophic Manuscripts*, p. 300.
[2] Ibid. 309.

producer—in order to sneak for himself a few pieces of silver ... He puts himself at the service of the other's most depraved fancies, plays the pimp between him and his need, excites in him morbid appetites.[3]

Later, Marx adds: 'Industry speculates on the refinement of needs, it speculates however just as much on their *crudeness*, whose true enjoyment, therefore, is *self-stupefaction*—this *illusory* satisfaction of need—this civilization contained within the crude barbarism of need.'[4]

The idea that people may be bound and blind to their oppression has come to be increasingly important in the Marxist tradition. It is central to the theories of both Lukács and Lenin, for instance, that the spontaneous consciousness of the workers does not coincide with their true or genuine class consciousness. Lukács says that their spontaneous consciousness, 'the consciousness of their existence that men have at any given time',[5] although 'subjectively justified in the social and historical situation',[6] is objectively a 'false consciousness'.[7] He adds:

the naive description of what men *in fact* thought, felt and wanted at any moment in history and from any given point in the class structure ... remains after all merely the *material* of genuine historical analysis ... By relating consciousness to the whole of society it becomes possible to infer the thoughts and feelings which men would have in a particular situation if they were *able* to assess both it and the interests arising from it in their impact on immediate action and on the whole structure of society. That is to say, it would be possible to infer the thoughts and feelings appropriate to their objective situation ... Now class consciousness consists in fact of the appropriate and rational reactions 'imputed' to a particular typical position in the process of production. This consciousness is, therefore, neither the sum nor the average of what is thought and felt by the single individuals who make up the class.[8]

Obviously, one can be more or less pessimistic about the

---

[3] Ibid. 306–7.
[4] Ibid, 311.
[5] Lukács, *History and Class Consciousness*, p. 50.
[6] Ibid.
[7] Ibid.
[8] Ibid. 51.

size of what Lukács calls 'the gap between the psychological consciousness and the imputed one',[9] and the possibility of closing it. In *History and Class Consciousness* he seems to have thought that, although it could not be guaranteed, it is at any rate possible for the proletariat to overcome the 'devastating and degrading effects of the capitalist system upon its class consciousness'.[10] For Lenin, the spontaneous consciousness of the workers was trade unionist and therefore already relatively mature; he also thought that the workers could be diverted from their spontaneous trade union inclinations and brought to an awareness of the necessity for class struggle by professional revolutionaries. But other Marxists have been more pessimistic both in respect of the distance between the workers' perceived and ascribed interests, and the possibility of bridging it. Marcuse, for instance, is conspicuously less hopeful. In *One-Dimensional Man* we find a gloomy picture of advanced industrial society as exerting massive control over the consciousness of its members, via the 'manipulation of needs'[11] and implantation of illusory modes of gratification, so that the possibility of opposition is effectively obliterated. The former antagonists in the class struggle are said by Marcuse now to be united, because

The productive apparatus and the goods and services which it produces 'sell' or impose the social system as a whole. The means of mass transportation and communication, the commodities of lodging, food, and clothing, the irresistible output of the entertainment and information industry carry with them prescribed attitudes and habits, certain intellectual and emotional reactions which bind the consumers more or less pleasantly to the producers and, through the latter, to the whole. The products indoctrinate and manipulate; they promote a false consciousness which is immune against its falsehood ... Thus emerges a pattern of *one-dimensional thought and behaviour* in which ideas, aspirations, and objectives that, by their content, transcend the established universe of discourse and action are either repelled or reduced to terms of this universe.[12]

Of course, the belief that it is possible to question or attack

[9] Lukács, *History and Class Consciousness*, p. 74.
[10] Ibid. 80.
[11] Marcuse, *One-dimensional Man*, p. 3.
[12] Ibid. 11–12.

people's versions of what is good or desirable for them is not unique to Marxism. There are many other theories which share with it the belief that people can be wrong in identifying with the values of a dominant group, the only difference being that they do not necessarily conceive of that group in class or economic terms. Marxists believe that the proletariat loses sight of its interests to the extent that its aims and aspirations are contaminated by the ideology of the bourgeois class. Black consciousness critics in South Africa believe that blacks who identify with the cultural values of whites rather than the indigenous, traditional values of African culture do themselves psychological damage. And feminists believe that women who have digested the patriarchal world-view have been cramped and crushed. The examples could be multiplied. I want to leave these details behind and turn to the underlying philosophical assumptions shared by all such views. They are, first, that there is a fact of the matter about what is good for people, and second, that it may not be good for people to get what they want. I am going to argue in this chapter that both of those assumptions are true.

2. SOME THEORIES

I said in the last section that the idea of proletarian false consciousness presupposes that what is good or desirable for people is both a factual matter and independent of their desires. But it might be wondered if these are really different claims. Surely, it may be objected, if what is good for you does not coincide with what you want, that must be because what is good for you is an objective matter. In which case, there are not, after all, two claims here, but only one—not different theses but the same thought alternatively formulated.

David Wiggins relies quite heavily on something like the assumption embedded in this objection in his British Academy lecture, 'Truth, Invention, and the Meaning of Life'. In that lecture he objects to Richard Taylor's idea that what could transform a meaningless into a meaningful existence is mere desire to do what was previously thought to have no meaning. Suppose, says Wiggins, that Sisyphus were to come to want to roll stones forever. This could not, he argues, give Sisyphus's, activities a value they did not have before, mainly because you could not accept that that was what gave your life meaning and still believe your life had meaning. For the will 'picks and chooses, deliberates, weighs concerns. It craves objective reasons; and often it could not go forward unless it thought it had them.'[13] I agree with what Wiggins says here and in fact I supply other arguments later which support his view (see Ch. III. 7). But Wiggins thinks his argument has an implication which it does not have: he thinks that in demonstrating the falsity of Taylor's account of what gives life value, he has refuted a non-cognitive account of valuations, a non-cognitive account being one which claims that valuations or value-judgements are not supplied by the intellect and cannot be true or false. He says:

Scarcely very tendentiously, I shall call Taylor's and all similar doctrines non-cognitive accounts of the meaning of life. For non-cognitivists have always resembled Taylor in striving for descriptions of the human condition by which will and intellect-cum-perception are kept separate and innocent of all dubious or inside transactions. The intellect supplies uncontaminated factual perception, deduction, and means-end reasoning. Ends are supplied (in this picture) by feeling or will.[14]

Presumably Wiggins connects the thought that desire confers value with the thought that value-judgements cannot be true or false, because he is reasoning like this: 'Non-cognitivists would be right that value-judgements cannot be true or false if value-judgements did not state facts but expressed subjective states like attitudes or desires. But I have shown that value does not reside in the satisfaction of subjective states like desires. So what value-judgements express cannot be something subjective or in ourselves, and there must accordingly be objective reasons why we should choose one way of life rather than another.' The mistake in this reasoning is in the assumption that an argument about the nature of *value* has repercussions for the nature of value-*judgements*. In fact it does not, and a theory about the nature of the

---

[13] Wiggins, 'Truth, Invention, and the Meaning of Life', p. 341.
[14] Ibid. 340.

one does not commit you to a theory about the nature of the other.

Consider the analogous relationship, or, rather, lack of relationship, between questions about morality and questions about moral judgements. The latter are about the status of ethics and the former about its content.[15] When we are interested in the status of ethics we are interested in the nature of the practice of making moral judgements: are we, in making moral judgements, imparting information or are we rather expressing something like an attitude, inclination, or desire? These are semantic issues. By contrast, when we are interested in the content of ethics, we are concerned with very different, normative or substantive, questions—what is right and wrong and what matters morally. And the important thing to see is that a view about the one does not commit you to a view about the other, that the semantic theory says nothing about the first-order questions.

Consider the non-cognitivist view that moral judgements do not have truth-conditions and that there is no objective basis for choosing between one set of moral principles and another. Does this view have any first-order implications? It might be thought that it must erode conviction on first-order matters. But, in fact, there is no connection between non-cognitivism and an attitude of indifference to moral questions. The reason, as Bernard Williams says, is that a non-cognitivist thinks that 'disagreement in morality involves what should be done, and involves, on each side, caring about what happens; and once you see this . . . you see equally that it could not possibly be a requirement of rationality that you should stop caring about these things because someone else disagrees with you'.[16] A connected way in which non-cognitivists may justify their interest in morality is to point out that it would be as silly to stop caring about moral issues because there is no objective resolution of them as to stop caring about what you eat because judgements of taste do not have truth-conditions.

'But isn't it at least the case that non-cognitivists about moral judgements must be relativists about first-order ques-

---

[15] This is Mackie's terminology in the Preface to his *Ethics*, p. 9.
[16] Williams, *Morality*, p. 48.

tions, and believe that what is right and wrong varies, and depends on what each individual takes to be right and wrong?' Even this is not true. For one thing, non-cognitivism does not as such imply any great variability in moral judgements. The reason is that it is quite possible for non-cognitivists to believe that we are all so constructed as to favour or approve of the same things. And if we share the same sentiments by virtue of a common nature, responding identically to actions, events, and qualities of character, our moral opinions will agree, not differ. But even if we do not share the same reactions, non-cognitivists do not have to believe that what is right and wrong varies. On the contrary, they can believe as firmly as anyone else that some moral views are acceptable, others appalling and obnoxious. For, as Simon Blackburn has shown, judgements that are not expressions of belief may nevertheless share syntactic and other features with judgements that are. So someone who believes that moral properties are merely projections on to nature of our sentiments or subjective attitudes may nevertheless think that the realistic-appearing nature of our moral discourse is justified, and involves no fraud.[17] A non-cognitivist can hold as strongly as anyone else that the right thing to do is maximize happiness, and any other attitude is wrong. Or that certain absolute rules and duties should be observed, and that any other attitude is wrong. Or whatever. The point is that non-cognitivism is compatible with non-relativist first-order moral theories.

To come back now to Wiggins and what makes a way of life worthwhile: Wiggins is attacking the normative theory that the *locus* or source of value is the satisfaction of wants—that is, the theory that what is good for you must coincide with what you want. He thinks that the success of his attack implies the truth of the semantic theory that judgements about what is worthwhile are objective. But I think we can see now that someone could combine Wiggins's distaste for the normative view that only human states of satisfaction have value with the opposite semantic theory, believing that the normative views about value shared with Wiggins are not expressions of belief, but

---

[17] Blackburn, *Spreading the Word*, ch. 6.

rather of subjective states. In other words, that desire does not confer value can be an attitude, not a belief. Conversely, someone could reject Wiggins's normative view while agreeing with him that value-judgements are objective. Bentham might be an example.

I said originally that Marxism is committed to two claims, namely that what is good for people is a factual matter and that what is good for them may not coincide with what they want. And I think that I have said enough to show that these are indeed different claims and not alternative ways of expressing the same thought. One is semantic, the other normative, and there are possible views on which only one is accepted and the other denied. There are really four possibilities:

1. There is a fact of the matter about interests and they consist in the satisfaction of wants.
2. There is a fact of the matter about interests and they do not consist in the satisfaction of wants.
3. There is not a fact of the matter about interests and they consist in the satisfaction of wants.
4. There is not a fact of the matter about interests and they do not consist in the satisfaction of wants.

Of course, proponents of the third and fourth views would not believe that they could show that interests consist in, or do not consist in, the satisfaction of desires, but that does not mean that their position is inconsistent. After all, I cannot show that chocolate cake is better than carrot cake but that is no reason for me not to prefer it.

So far I have been very schematic about the two claims implied by the Marxist attack on the proletariat's spontaneous consciousness and its ideologically contaminated desires. Now I must say a bit more about what they involve. It is best to begin with what I described, rather roughly, as the claim that what is good for agents may not be what they want. I shall say that a theory which makes this claim has a want-independent conception of interests. It asserts that the desirability of a state of affairs depends on what is best for people whatever they may happen to want; it depends on the wants they ought to

have, whether they actually have them or not.[18] This is still a
bit inexact, however, for even on the opposing, want-based,
conception of interests, there is a sense in which interests
come apart from wants. A man wants to step on to a bridge
but his belief that it is sturdy is false, to adapt an example of
Mill's.[19] No one would say that it is in his interests to step on to
the bridge; so the want-based conception, which says that what
is in people's interests is what would best satisfy their wants,
needs a stricter formulation.

It will not do to say that if the man steps on to the bridge, he
does not get what he wants, because there is an obvious sense
in which he does. But what is true is that he does not want to
step on to the bridge under the description 'unsafe bridge'.
The point is that desires are intentional. It can be true both
that you want to step on to the bridge and that the bridge is
broken, without its being true that you want to step on to the
broken bridge. The want-based conception can help itself to
this fact about the intentionality of desire to make the exact
connection it needs between wants and interests. It can say
that your interests are satisfied when the results you expect to
come about from doing what you desire in fact come about.
This accommodates all the cases in which, due to some
deficiency in your knowledge or reasoning, what you want is
not in your interests or what is in your interests you do not
want. There is the case where you have a false belief about the
object of your desire, and there are other, similar, sorts of case
too. You may have forgotten some element which would have
influenced your deliberations had you remembered it; or
perhaps you have a false belief about the cost to you of getting
what you want. The important thing about all such cases is
that the want-based conception gets at what is in the agent's
interests by putting the facts to work on ends which the agent
actually has. Strictly speaking, what it puts to work on those
ends is all the information which would make a difference in
the agent's deliberations if proper use were made of it. I shall

[18] I owe this way of putting it to Brian Barry, who calls this sort of theory an
'ideal-regarding' theory of interests. See his *Political Argument*, pp. 38–40.

[19] Mill, *On Liberty*, pp. 228–9.

continue to speak loosely, however, and say that the format for the want-based conception is: existing motivation plus the facts. The combination tells you how to satisfy your interests but only because it is already known what you expect to achieve.

So on the want-based conception, the only way in which interests can come apart from desires is if you lack or fail to use information relevant to your deliberations. There is no question of your desires being *intrinsically* defective. A desire which survives the impact of the facts is beyond criticism. This is part of what Hume meant when he said that 'Reason is . . . the slave of the passions, and can never pretend to any other office than to serve and obey them'.[20]

On a want-independent conception of interests, by contrast, what is in your interests has no necessary connection with what you want, or even with what you would want if you knew the facts. It follows that, even if your desire is not based on false belief, it is possible, on the want-independent conception, that its fulfilment might not be good for you. This would be the case with an intrinsically bad desire. Conversely, on this conception, some goods are objectively goods, irrespective of your desires.

The first of the claims implied by Marxism is that interests are not want-based. The second is that judgements about interests, about what is good for people, are factual and express beliefs. The view opposed to this is that judgements about interests are expressions of affective states like attitudes or desires, and therefore cannot be true or false.

Finally, I must say something about two other issues which are relevant here, although I have not mentioned them yet. The first is this. So far I have suggested that the claim that workers suffer from false consciousness implies, in part, that the fulfilment of their desires may not be good for them, or, in other words, that interests are not want-based. This is a natural interpretation, but there is also a more arcane possibility, which is that the idea behind an ascription of false consciousness is rather that those who suffer from it do not 'truly' want

---

[20] Hume, *A Treatise of Human Nature*, II. iii. 3.

what they think they want, the underlying idea being that if something is not good for you, and you believe you want it, your belief must be false. In other words, the idea behind an ascription of false consciousness would be that wants are interest-based, not that interests are want-based.

The second issue which I must mention here, also in an introductory sort of way, concerns the relationship of perceptions of interests to action. The reason it arises in this context is that Marxists sometimes assert that although people who have absorbed ideological values get what they want, they would have different desires if only they knew where their interests lay. Their desires have nothing to do with determining their interests, for their interests are established independently of their desires, but once the facts about their interests are known, it is said the desires must follow on. It seems that Lukács believed something like this, for it will be remembered that he said that genuine class consciousness consists in the thoughts and feelings which agents would have if they were able properly to assess their situation. Notice that although both this theory and the want-based theory of interests have in common that they trade in the wants people would have if they knew the facts, this theory differs in supposing that when people come to want what is good for them, it is *because* it is good for them that they want it. It is not because they want it, or would want it, that it is good for them.

It will be quickly seen that the assertion I have described presupposes a particular view of the relationship of perceptions of interests to action, namely that judgements about interests necessarily motivate or move to action. It implies that to judge that something would be in your interests is necessarily to acquire at least the inclination to act in a way that conforms to the judgement. Now the view that judgements about interests or prudential judgements are necessarily practical is truistic when combined with the view that prudential judgements are the expression of an attitude or desire. For, evidently, it is in the nature of attitudes or desires that they should incline the agent to action. But it is highly controversial when combined with the Marxist view that judgements about interests are factual. For then it amounts to the claim that a *belief* about interests has motivational force. And that violates the natural assumption that no cognitive state can, on its own, be motivationally efficacious.[21]

It might be wondered if that is such a natural assumption. After all, is it not a feature of our experience that sensitive use of the intellect and imagination can provoke new patterns of motivation and extinguish the old? Yes, but again it is natural to think that when that happens the intellect and the imagination are not working in a vacuum but on a pre-existing motivational structure. Someone in favour of capital punishment might, for instance, be brought to oppose it, but only, it seems, if we have managed to engage her sympathies. Or someone might find his desire to avenge an injustice diminished if he is brought to see that it is preventing him from pursuing his other projects. But it seems our appeal will have been to a mixture of facts and a rival desire, the desire of the man to see his aims accomplished. In the absence of the competing desire, how could there be reason for him to forget the wrong done him? But if what you can come to care about itself requires some input from your desires, then the natural assumption that beliefs about facts cannot on their own be a source of motivation *has* been brought into play.

I said earlier that part of what Hume meant when he said that reason is the slave of the passions is that reason cannot pronounce on the value of desires. I think that the rest of what he meant by that dictum is captured by the natural assumption just described. These tend not to be distinguished, although they are different claims, and one could—and, I shall be arguing, should—accept the one and not the other. One claim is that reason cannot disclose an intrinsic defect in a desire, and I shall argue that that is false. The other is that reason cannot on its own motivate or provoke desire, and I shall argue that that is true. But that is to anticipate.

---

[21] There is a stronger and a weaker claim in this area, as Michael Smith has pointed out. The stronger claim is that non-cognitive states are an essential *source* of motivation; the weaker claim is that a non-cognitive state is always *present* when there is motivated behaviour. (See 'The Humean Theory of Motivation', pp. 36–7). It is weaker because it could be uninterestingly true. This would be so, as Thomas Nagel has pointed out, if the presence of the non-cognitive state is itself explained by something cognitive (see *The Possibility of Altruism*, pp. 29–31). The natural assumption I have mentioned embodies the stronger claim.

I have now described four issues suggested by the idea of proletarian false consciousness. The first is whether 'interest' is a want-based concept; the second, whether there is a fact of the matter about interests; the third, whether 'desire' is an interest-based concept; and the fourth, whether judgements about interests necessarily motivate. It is clear that if we combine the different views on these issues we shall get a number of theories. Their relationship to one another can be represented diagrammatically as in Table 3.1.

I need not discuss each of these combinations separately because, clearly, an argument to the effect that, say, perceptions of interests have no necessary connection with the will would rule out not only B but also E and H. And an argument that interests are not want-based would dispose of not only D, but also E and F. It will therefore be enough in what follows to discuss the theories represented in Table 3.2.

I have called one theory 'realism' to draw attention to its affinities with what is called 'moral realism', which is the view that moral facts provide reasons for action. The idea is that we recognize morally desirable features in the world and the recognition of moral desirability brings the appropriate motivation along with it.[22] Moral realism, in other words, has the best of both worlds, if it is true. For it lays claim to both objectivity and motivational force for moral judgements. The theory I am interested in is imperialistic in the same way, wanting to commandeer, as it does, both objectivity and motivational force for judgements about interests.

The theory I have called 'subjectivism' also has two faces, being a theory not only about interests—which it claims to be want-based—but also about prudential judgements—which it claims to be non-factual. But it might be doubted whether the name I have given is appropriate. For it is not clear that both claims are subjectivist claims. Certainly the one about prudential judgements is. But how, it might be asked, is the claim that interests are want-based any less objectivist than the claim that they are not want-based? Surely they both give objective answers to the question about what interests consist in? Moreover (the objector might go on), if what you desire to achieve is

---

[22] See Nagel, *The Possibility of Altruism*, pp. 80–1.

TABLE 3.1

	Interests are want-independent	Interests are want-based	Wants are interest-based
Prudential judgements express beliefs			
Perception of interests is not necessarily practical	A	D	G
Perception of interests is necessarily practical	B	E	H
Prudential judgements express desires	C	F	

TABLE 3.2

	Interests are want-independent	Interests are want-based	Wants are interest-based
Prudential judgements express beliefs	Perception of interests is not necessarily practical	Reductionism		True want theory
	Perception of interests is necessarily practical	Realism		
Prudential judgements express desires			Subjectivism	

known, then on the want-based theory it is an objective matter what you should do. In which case, the theory I have called 'subjectivism' mixes subjectivist and objectivist components and is therefore misleadingly named.

I think there are three points which can be made apropos of this doubt, considerations which show that 'subjectivism' is not a misnomer. First, although it is true that the question 'What is good for us?' receives a fixed and constant answer on the want-based conception of interests—namely, 'Whatever we want'—since we want different things we can never, on that conception of interests, *agree* on what things are good for us. Second, the want-based conception has no place for the concept of an intrinsically defective desire. Third, the fact that given your desires it is an objective matter what it is best for you to do does not imply that it is an objective matter what it is best for you to do, any more than the fact that it is an objective matter which terrier is best, given our standards for judging terriers, implies that it is an objective matter which terrier is best. Because the choice of standards for judging terriers is essentially arbitrary, there is no answer to the question which terrier is best as such. And since, on the want-based conception of interests, desires are as immune to criticism as standards for judging dogs, there is likewise no answer to the question of what it is non-relatively best for someone to do. So both elements of the theory I have called 'subjectivism' are subjectivist, and the theory is not misleadingly named.

Then there is the true want theory, which says that you only truly want what it is in your interests you should get.

And finally there is the theory I have called 'reductionism', which aims to re-express the content of judgements about interests in another vocabulary, a natural vocabulary; it also holds that beliefs about such ordinary matters of fact are not action-guiding, thus implying that it is possible for people not to want what is good for them even when they know what that is. As we have seen, the realist theory about the relationship between desire and cognition shares with the want-based theory about interests the thesis that the only circumstances in which agents can fail to satisfy their interests is if there is a cognitive deficit. By contrast, reductionism allows for another kind of shortcoming, for it allows that even when agents know the facts about what is good for them, their desires may fail to correspond. In fact, I shall argue that in failing to sever the connection here, between knowledge and desire, the realist theory has a problem. Of course, both theories, realism and reductionism, are controversial in claiming that what is good for us is a matter of fact; but realism has an extra problem in the idea that knowledge of what is good for us elicits matching motivation.

I should mention that some of these theories do not necessarily imply a position on all the issues distinguished. The essential features of realism, for instance, derive from its stance on the motivation issue and the issue about the objectivity of prudential judgements, and it is really essentially neutral on the question about the correct conception of interests. Likewise, a reductionist theory could hold that the natural facts to which the facts about interests are reducible are facts about people's desires, and a true want theory could hold that perceptions of interests are necessarily practical. However, I am going to argue that the want-based conception of interests is flawed and that cognitive states cannot, on their own, be motivationally efficacious. That is why, on the diagram, I have represented realism, reductionism, and the true want theory as committed to a position on the issues in which they are not essentially interested. I have attributed to them what I believe is the right answer to those questions, so that they should appear at their most plausible, not at their least.

My strategy in the next few sections will be this. I shall argue against the true want theory first. Then I shall argue that the realist view of the relationship between desire and cognition is wrong. Next I shall argue against the truth of the subjectivist thesis about the non-factual nature of prudential judgements, and finally against the truth of the one about the want-based nature of interests. The truth of reductionism will have been demonstrated and the upshot will be that the assumptions behind the idea of false consciousness, at least if it is not interpreted in the esoteric, 'true want' way, are philosophically defensible.

3. TRUE WANTS

The true want theory asserts that agents whose goals and aspirations have been corrupted by ideological influences do not 'truly' or 'really' want what they think they want, the underlying idea being that you only truly want what it is in your interests to get or what is good for you. So people whose actions are informed by ideologically influenced goals mis-identify their desires, and what they really want is to pursue entirely different projects. Obviously, the nature of these projects will differ, depending on the specification of what is in the individual's interests. In the case of Marxism, the good life is said to be enjoyed by those who have achieved the richest development of personality. But there is nothing to stop alternative visions of the good life from accompanying the belief that agents only truly want what is objectively good for them.

There is some textual evidence for the true want theory in Marx—remember the '*imaginary* appetites' of which he spoke in the *Economic and Philosophic Manuscripts*—and the idea has a powerful intellectual ancestry. Plato, for instance, argued that the true object of everyone's wants is the just life. The bad man's wants, said Plato, are unreal or less real, his pleasures being merely the cessation of pains. Again, Rousseau claimed that since what is of fundamental importance to us is found in the public domain, if we act on private concerns our real desires are not fulfilled and our will is merely 'apparent'. And Hegel's 'great man of the age' is 'the one who can put into words the will of his age, tell his age what its will is and accomplish it'.[23]

One way to clarify the claim of the true want theory and to assess its plausibility is to see what is involved in the kind of mistake about a desire that it postulates, and how this differs from what is involved in some other kinds of mistake about desires that other theories postulate. Of course, any theory which allows for you to misidentify your desires can be called

[23] Hegel, *Philosophy of Right*, addition to § 318.

a 'true want theory', but for clarity's sake I shall reserve the name for a species of that genus, namely the theory which claims that such a misidentification occurs when your desires make you worse off. I shall argue that it makes no sense of the concept of desire.

There are interesting and uninteresting uses of the notion of a true want. Consider, for instance, the use to which it is put by John Harsanyi his a paper, 'Morality and the Theory of Rational Behavior'. He distinguishes in that paper between a person's 'manifest' and 'true' preferences. He calls 'manifest' a person's 'actual preferences as manifested by his observed behavior, including preferences possibly based on erroneous factual beliefs, or on careless logical analysis, or on strong emotions that at the moment greatly hinder rational choice'. And he calls 'true' the preferences a person '*would* have if he had all the relevant information, always reasoned with the greatest possible care, and were in a state of mind most con-ducive to rational choice'.[24] What I want to point out is that there can be no suggestion here that when your manifest preference diverges from your true preference, you are in any way in error about your manifest preference. You would want to do something else if you had all the relevant information, reasoned with the greatest possible care, and so on, but you are not wrong about what you want to do now. You do not *misidentify* your actual or manifest desire. In fact, Harsanyi's is merely a flamboyant way of making the point that we have already seen the want-based theory about interests make, namely that sometimes agents want something which they wouldn't want were it not for their false belief that it is a means to a desired end. Harsanyi puts this quite extravagantly, by saying that the agent only truly wants what actually is the means to the desired end (Mill's man, wanting to cross to the other side, does not 'truly' want to step on the broken bridge), but since this agent has made no mistake about his *desires*, but only about the facts, it is at best trivial to talk in these terms. (At worst, it is misleading, for the use of the expression 'true' is actually an inaccurate way of getting at the discrepancy

[24] Harsanyi, 'Morality and the Theory of Rational Behaviour', p. 55.

between what the agent expects and what actually happens, there being nothing that the so-called true preference matches.)

Harsanyi's is a trivial use of the expression 'true want'. If it is to be interestingly used, we must look for cases where agents misidentify their desires, cases which require the introduction of such distinctions as that between the manifest and the latent, and which call for the idea of uncovering or unmasking. One hypothesis which implies the existence of such cases is Freud's, namely the hypothesis of unconscious mental activity. Freud's idea is that a wish can need a disguise. The disguise is an avowed desire; it covers for the unavowable or unconscious desire, and the latter, being the operative desire, is the real or true desire. An example is the ritual of Freud's patient who many times a day on some pretext rang for the maid, so arranging things that the maid would see a stain on the table-cloth, which stood proxy for the wish that her husband had not been impotent on the wedding-night.

Freud's hypothesis is clearly a way of making sense of the notion of what is really or truly wanted. However, it is not a way open to someone who would like to say that those whose desires have been influenced by ideology are in error about what they want. This is so for two main reasons. The first turns on the fact that the desires under discussion are desires such as those singled out by Marx in his attack on the 'morbid appetites' for the consumer products made available by private enterprise. Agents are *victims* of these desires. The whole point about them is that they are desires whose fulfilment is said to bring the individual no benefit. Now the true want theory claims that the individual does not really want what brings no benefit. But it may not help itself to the hypothesis of unconscious mental activity and locate the true desire in another, inaccessible part of the mind. Freud could, because the sort of error he discovered is intelligible, the misconstrual being in some sense functional for the subject. Repression or symptom formation is, according to Freud, a way of warding off anxiety. This is why Freud talks of a 'flight into illness': there is a gain from the misidentification of the desire. But there is no gain in the ideological case where, as I have just explained, the experienced desire by hypothesis serves no interest, or no interest of the subject at any rate. It is others who benefit from the supposed mistake.

This is really the big difference between the desires and motivations which are the subject of this chapter, and the desires and motivations canvassed in the last one. There the claim that the beliefs of the bourgeoisie about their motives are false made immediate sense, for those beliefs *cater* to class interest. They legitimate class activities. And because there is something to be gained from them, I was entitled to argue, as I did, that the useful beliefs could be the outcome of an unconscious plan. But here we are dealing with people who pursue goals which *frustrate* their interests. They are said to identify with and aspire to what makes them worse off. If their beliefs about their desires are also false, as the true want theorist claims, then that cannot be because their real desires are inaccessible to consciousness. Precisely because the false belief, if there is one, brings no benefit, the hypothesis of unconscious mental activity cannot get a grip here. In a nutshell: in Freud the operative desire is expelled from consciousness because it is painful and it is replaced in consciousness by a symptom which serves a function. By contrast, in the ideological case the so-called true desire is not painful—indeed, in so far as one can make sense of the idea, the opposite is the case—and there is therefore no reason for it to be dispatched to another, inaccessible, part of the mind.

I said there was a second reason why the hypothesis of unconscious mental activity does not match the facts about ideological desires, apart from the consideration that there is nothing to be gained from the expulsion of the desire from consciousness. The reason Freud is entitled to say that the unconscious desire is the real one is because it is the desire that explains the agent's neurotic behaviour. How are we to explain the fact that at one moment the Rat Man is obliged to remove a stone from the road and at the next to replace it, unless we bring in his unconscious desire to harm his lady? In the ideological case, by contrast, there is no explanatory work for the so-called real desire to do. If the appetite for 'every new product' is merely imaginary, as Marx says, that is not because there is some non-imaginary desire which explains what individuals pursue. *Ex hypothesi*, it is the 'imaginary' desire which moves them, whereas the so-called real desire, the desire for what would do them good, is a fiction, not the prime mover or author of behaviour. The real desire makes no difference to what they do; it is not *in them* at all.

There is a theory about desire which comes a bit closer than Freud's to what the true want theorist needs. It is the theory put forward by Russell in *The Analysis of Mind.* There he says that we identify a desire by what brings a feeling of satisfaction or the cessation of discomfort: if you believe you want something, but get no satisfaction from it, your belief was false and you were wrong about your desire. 'If our theory of desire is correct', he says, 'a belief as to its purpose may very well be erroneous, since only experience can show what causes a discomfort to cease.'[25]

There are problems with this which I shall come to shortly, but it is worth investigating the direction in which the true want theorist would have to push it. It is a fact about ideological desires, which the true want theorist must accommodate, that people who are seduced by ideological values often get what they go after and feel satisfied with what they sought. Notice that these need not coincide, there being an important difference between the fulfilment of a desire and its satisfaction.[26] A desire is fulfilled when the state of the world which is wanted comes about. A desire is satisfied when the desirer experiences a pleasant mental state on account of believing the desire fulfilled. Now the fact that people who are seduced by the dominant values of their society often achieve their aims is one of the reasons why the true want theorist has to be making a different claim from the trivial claim about true wants which I talked about earlier. The trivial claim relies on the fact that people's wants may be based on false beliefs, with the obvious consequence that things backfire on them rather than going according to plan. It says, trivially, that wants based on false beliefs are not 'true'. But the true want theory has to make room for the notion of a true want even where things do go according to plan. Its distinctive, non-trivial claim is that even when what is expected is actually obtained, your

[25] B. Russell, *The Analysis of Mind*, p. 72.
[26] Feinberg, 'Harm and Self-Interest', p. 62.

belief that you *wanted* what you expected to obtain may be false. The point I want to make here is that although Russell's analysis does make the non-trivial claim that you could have misidentified your desire despite getting what you expected, it still does not go quite far enough for the true want theorist. For according to Russell we identify a desire by what brings a feeling of satisfaction, but the true want theory has to allow for the misidentification of desire even where you *do not* feel disappointed with what you get, for it is a fact about ideological desires that they are not made less ideological when their fulfilment brings satisfaction. Remember the 'self-stupefaction' about which Marx talked, the enjoyment which comes from the satisfaction of 'unnatural appetites'. So the true want theory cannot simply take over Russell's criterion of desire, namely that it brings a feeling of satisfaction. It has to say that even when agents do get satisfaction from obtaining what they think they want, their beliefs about their desires can be false. The underlying reason is that, in Russell, psychical integrity is at least intact, whereas, according to Marxists, ideology has an impact on and tampers with the mind. A good analogy for what is suggested by Marxists is hypnosis. People under the influence of post-hypnotic suggestion may derive satisfaction from bizarre activities. Suppose you have been hypnotized to get satisfaction from eating coal. Then satisfaction loses any plausibility it might have had as the sole clue to your desires.

So signs of satisfaction *à la* Russell are not quite enough for the true want theorist's analysis of desire. On the other hand, what we find in Russell is certainly quite close to the true want theorist's idea that what is really wanted is what is good for you, for what is good for you must satisfy, even if not all that satisfies can be said to be really wanted. So satisfaction must figure in at least an indirect way in the true want theorist's account of desire.

There is a way of making it figure quite directly, and consequently of reducing the difference between Russell's and the true want theory, and that is if the true want theory claims that people can be wrong about feeling satisfied, in just the way that they can be wrong about what they want. It would then be claiming that they are only really satisfied when they get what

is good for them. But whether it says that agents are only satisfied when they get what they really want, or merely that when
agents get what they really want they are satisfied, it is in
trouble. It is not true that what is really wanted always brings
satisfaction in its train, for desires just do not have that kind of
connection with feelings. For one thing, there is often no
reason to think that someone who wants something is aiming
at a pleasant mental state; we want many things which we
expect not to enjoy. An example of James Griffin's makes this
point: Freud refused to take analgesics towards the end of his
life, wanting rather to think in pain than to be in a pleasant
but muddled state of mind.[27] It is also the case that even when
we *do* aim at a feeling of contentment or something similar,
there is no guarantee that fulfilment of the desire will bring
the feeling with it. The point is that though you get what you
really want, you can still be disappointed. And it certainly does
not follow from your disappointment that you were wrong
about the object of your desire. Examples range from the
neurotic to the commonplace—from the character-type Freud
described as 'wrecked by success'[28] to the husband and wife
who waste their wishes in the fairy tale.[29]

Pears points out that it is needs, not desires, which have a
connection with what is satisfying.[30] If you believe you are
hungry, but eating brings no satisfaction, then you have taken
a sensation of discomfort to signal a need which it does not
signal: you have misidentified a need.[31] Needs are determined
by a 'psychological investigation of the person's original constitution'; desires are determined through behaviour.[32] This is

[27] Griffin, 'Are There Incommensurable Values?', p. 43.
[28] Freud, 'Some Character-Types Met with in Psycho-Analytic Work', Standard Edition, xiv. 263.
[29] There are many versions of the tale. One of them is this: 'A rogue catches a goblin who grants him three wishes, two of which the man gives to his wife. But while they are eating a marrow bone for dinner, and having difficulty extracting the marrow, the wife unthinkingly wishes her husband had the beak of a wood-cock. The husband, infuriated at finding himself with a long beak on the front of his face, wishes his wife may have one too. They sit there both with their long beaks; with two of their three wishes already used; and with "no good gained thereby". It is obvious to both of them what their last wish will have to be.' (Opie and Opie, *The Classic Fairy Tales*, p. 196.)
[30] Pears, 'Russell's Theory of Desire', in *Questions in the Philosophy of Mind*, p. 262.
[31] Ibid. 259.
[32] Ibid. 262.

really what is so strange about the true want theory: it says
that what is really willed is what is good for you, whether you
aim at that in your behaviour or not. But that is an impossible
theory about desire. For it is essential to our concept of a
desire that desires should seek, through behaviour, to be fulfilled.

I conclude from all this that though other theories—notably
Freud's—may work intelligibly with the notion of true wants,
the Marxist claim that people are wrong about what is good
for them cannot be read as a claim to the effect that they are
wrong about what they want. Leaving aside the question
whether it can be true to say that people are mistaken about
what is good for them—I show in Ch. III. 5 that it can—the
upshot of the present argument is that it is impossible to
reinterpret such a mistake, a mistake about what is good for
you, as a mistake about desires.

But perhaps it will be objected that I have not been fair to
the true want theory, for it only implies the impossible conclusion that agents want what does not move them and do not
want what does, if you make the notion hang, as I have, on the
basing of wants on interests. But there are other possibilities.

For example, someone might argue as follows: 'True, the
fact that the satisfaction of an ideological desire does me no
good does not prevent it from being a *desire* of mine. But it
does not follow from the fact that the ideological desire is a
desire of mine that it is *my* desire, in anything other than the
trivial sense that I find it in me. And if it is not my desire, it is
not a *true* desire. It is interesting', my opponent continues, 'that
Rousseau, who often spoke in a way which made him susceptible to the kind of criticism levelled above—he talks, for
instance, of the 'blind multitude, which often does not know
what it wills, because it rarely knows what is good for it'[33]—at
other times seems to be claiming something closer to this new
interpretation. For there is also the idea in Rousseau that in
acting on the common purpose, which is the object of your
real will, you are not acting on anything foreign to yourself: in
obeying a law which conveys objective requirements of the
common interest, you are not dependent on other wills, but

[33] Rousseau, *The Social Contract*, p. 193.

on yourself only. In other words, Rousseau is here connecting your real desires with your identity, rather than with your interests.'

Or someone might argue as follows: 'There are some origins which are all wrong for desires. For instance, you might think it not true hunger if a neuro-physiologist causes the sensations of hunger in me by fiddling with my brain. Indeed, some psychologists have thought just that about the analogous phenomenon where, due to disease, people feel the sensations of hunger and thirst, although they are not suffering from lack of food or dehydration, and when they eat and drink they experience no satisfaction. Psychologists have thought it appropriate to call these sensations by the names "false hunger" and "false thirst".[34] Presumably the idea is that true hunger must be caused by a deficit; false hunger pretends to an origin it does not have. But then we can generalize and say that whenever the causation of a desire is fraudulent, the desire is not a true one, in the same way that a painting which pretends to be painted by Vermeer but is not, is not a true Vermeer. And ideological desires would easily fill *that* bill.'

In fact, I shall have quite a lot to say later, in Ch. IV. 1, about the 'ownership' of desires, and about whether its history can be a defect in a desire, but what I want to say now is that the notions of truth and falsity are misapplied in those contexts, for there is no point in saying that a desire which is not the agent's own, or a desire with a defective history, is not a true desire. Either it is just a metaphor, in which case the notion of truth bears no special weight anyway, or it is not, but then there would have to be some respect in which the desire has failed to match something, in a way analogous to that in which a false statement fails to fit the world, for that is at least what truth implies, but it is hard to see what respect that could be.

To sum up: read in a way which implies that wants are based on interests, the idea of a true want is unacceptable. There are other possible ways of reading the idea, but they abuse the notion of truth. The upshot is that the true want version of Marxism fails.

---

[34] David Pears described this phenomenon to me.

4. HOW DO PRUDENTIAL CONSIDERATIONS
   MOTIVATE US?

I want to deal now with the idea one finds in Lukács, that if
the victims of false consciousness were able truly to assess
their situation, they would come to have the 'appropriate and
rational reactions'. The philosophical view assumed here is the
realist view that there is a fact of the matter about what is
good for people and that acquaintance with such facts provokes action in accordance with them. Or rather, that is a
rough description of what it claims: a couple of refinements
are necessary.

For one thing, there is no need to burden realism with the
view that acquaintance with the facts about what is good for
you guarantees that you will act in the way that your interests
require. Some have taken that view, to be sure: it goes by the
name of 'psychological egoism' and Hobbes is perhaps its best-
known exponent. Famously, he denied that people are capable
of any motivation which is not self-interested. However, I need
to argue against realism at its most plausible, not at its least. So
I shall read it in its weaker form, as claiming that acquaintance
with the facts about what is good for you has a tendency,
merely, to provoke conforming action. (Moral realism might
have to make the more extravagant claim, for it is often
thought that moral considerations always override all others.
But I shall ignore that complication, since it is not really
relevant here.) Another way of putting this point is to say that
on the most plausible form of realism, prudential value-judgements provide only prima-facie, not all-things-considered,
reasons for action. A prima-facie judgement is one that an
action is desirable in so far as it has a certain characteristic. By
contrast, an all-things-considered judgement is one that the
desirable characteristic is enough to act on.[35]

But now it may be wondered whether realism is such an
ambitious doctrine after all. For surely, it may be asked, no one
would deny that if I put a positive valuation on some action I
have a *tendency* to go for it? It seems impossible that I should
say "What's my interest to me?"; that such considerations should

---

[35] Davidson, 'Intending', in *Essays on Actions and Events*, p. 98.

in general leave me stone cold, making for a complete dislocation between acknowledged interest and desire. The answer to this is that one can accept the impossibility but not interpret its basis in the way the realist does. It could just be a universal psychological tendency. By contrast, realism is committed to making the impossibility of someone's saying 'What's my interest to me?' a conceptual impossibility. For according to realism, judgements about interests have a necessary, not a contingent, connection with the will.

From here it is an easy step to recover what is distinctive about the theory. For it also holds that there is a fact of the matter about the inherently practical valuations. But that combination of features challenges what I earlier called the natural assumption that knowledge of the facts cannot on its own, or without some psychological input, force desire. The realist will have to show how it is possible that judgements about interests can both express beliefs and, in themselves, motivate.

E. J. Bond, in his book *Reason and Value*, believes it is possible but says little more in support of his view than that a desire *must* be elicited as a consequence of the cognition of value. It is worth remarking on the difference between this view and the more immediately intelligible claim which I discuss in the next section, that value-judgements express desires. Clearly, it is easy for the latter view to make the connection with action, for here the motivational force of value-judgements is guaranteed by the fact that they express action-disposing states. But on Bond's view, the value-judgement expresses a belief, so the connection with action is problematic.

Bond wants to agree with Hume that cognitions cannot motivate.[36] However, he also wants it to be the case that the intellect should determine the will. He thinks that the way to combine these is to argue that a cognition *generates* a desire.[37] But it is hard to see how this is a solution. It merely pushes the problem one stage back. If cognitions cannot move to action, then they cannot play the earlier role either, of generating desires, for desires are themselves action-disposing. The point

---

[36] Bond, *Reason and Value*, p. 68.
[37] Ibid. 12 and *passim*.

is that desires are already on the practical side of the progression from thought to action; so if there is a problem with cognitions causing actions, it must apply with respect to cognitions causing desires too. Conversely, if Bond is right that cognitive states can cause affective states, then that would refute Hume after all. For then the action would be explained by the perception of interests, not by the desire which is elicited by the perception.

Is Hume wrong? Can cognitions be the source of motivation? John McDowell argues in support of the view that they can. He claims, apropos of prudential judgements in particular, that if you are moved by considerations about your interests then it is enough to advert to your conception of the facts in order to explain the action you perform. In other words, your belief that acting in a certain way will serve your interests is in itself your reason for acting as you do. Any desire we ascribe to you, such as a desire for your own future happiness, is simply a consequence of the fact that you act for that reason and not an independent part of its explanation.[38] It follows that another could not have just that conception of the circumstances and yet see no reason to act as you do. So if you are unmoved by facts about your future interests, you must have a different understanding of the situation from someone who is so moved. McDowell says of the case where you cannot see how facts about your future can in themselves provide you with reasons for action, that you must have an 'idiosyncratic view' of what it is for a fact to concern your future. You might, for instance, view the person to whom the facts refer as someone whose connections with your present self are too tenuous to warrant concern.

What is special about a prudent version [person?] is a different understanding of what it is for a fact to concern his own future. He sees things otherwise in the relevant area; and we comprehend his prudent behaviour by comprehending the relevant fragment of his world view, not by appealing to the desire which is admittedly ascribable to him. That is to be understood, no less than the behaviour is, in terms of the world view.[39]

[38] McDowell, 'Are Moral Requirements Hypothetical Imperatives?', pp. 15–16. See also Nagel, *The Possibility of Altruism*, pp. 37–9.

[39] McDowell, 'Are Moral Requirements Hypothetical Imperatives?', p. 17.

I want to argue that McDowell is wrong and that the motivational force of a prudential judgement is not buried in the description alone. But before I do that I want to discuss an attack on the realist view which fails. Its author is G. R. Grice, in an article called 'Motive and Reason'. Grice uses two examples to make his points and it is probably best to begin with these. The first is this:

Suppose James is home from school for the summer holidays. It is a beautiful day and the river is at its best. One of James's delights is punting. His friends, home from other schools, are all going on the river, taking a picnic with them. There are girls in the party too, and James likes girls. But alas! he is in one of those dreadful moods of ennui. He is consumed with lethargy and as miserable as sin. He is in the kind of mood which we all know and which most of us sometimes suffer. He does not want to go on the river. All he wants to do is slouch around at home. Despite his lack of desire, we can suppose that he would enjoy it on the river if he would make the effort to conquer his present mood. We can suppose that he would enjoy it more than anything else he could do and certainly much more than a day spent moping. If this is so, there is good reason for his going on the river even though he does not want to. In staying at home, he is being stupid, foolish and unreasonable.[40]

Grice later goes on to say that if James knows the facts, it is not only the case that there is a reason for his going on the river; James also has a reason, although he may not have a motive.[41]

The second example is this:

Suppose a man of no talent and no financial resources is embarked upon a wretched career as an actor. He lives in poverty. He has no chance of success. He is thoroughly discontented and unhappy. It may be that despite his discontent and unhappiness, despite his poverty and the certainty of failure, he wants, and wants more than anything else, to persist in the life he has chosen. But it may also be that, despite his desires, and in addition to the facts cited, there are all sorts of hints to be found in his life that it is in his interest to tear himself away from the stage and sink himself in some other career.[42]

Grice takes these examples to show that the formula, 'No reason without a desire', is false. But before I can assess that

[40] Grice, 'Motive and Reason', p. 168.
[41] Ibid. 169.
[42] Ibid. 172.

claim, I must deal with a couple of complications. The first is that the formula can actually be read in two ways and Grice's attack on it is correspondingly ambiguous. He says that there can be reasons without desire but he slips between an interpretation of that claim according to which what you have reason to do does not depend on what you want, and an interpretation according to which what you have reason to do need not affect your desires. It is only the second of these that I am interested in at the moment, because it is the second that bears on the realist thesis, which asserts that a belief about what is in your interests elicits the relevant desire.

The second complication lies in the fact that Grice works with the concept of reasons. In fact, he means by 'there is a reason for someone to x' that 'x is in someone's interests', explicitly using these concepts interchangeably. For instance, he says that it is self-contradictory to say, 'It is in my interests to do x, but there is no reason for my doing x'.[43] But if he had confined himself to the notion of something's being in someone's interests, and not identified that with the concept of a reason to act, his argument would be less unstable than it is. The identification makes things even more difficult for Grice, the trouble being that however problematic the idea of divorcing judgements about interests from action, the idea of divorcing reasons to act from acting must be even more so. I shall be arguing later that you cannot split off reasons to act from action, that reasons do necessarily motivate. But for the moment, where the identification would matter, I shall read Grice's thesis as one about interests only and not about reasons, assuming that it is in that form that it is more likely to succeed.

Something which is more an oversight than a complication is the way in which Grice formulates the belief which he thinks false. He describes it as the belief that there is no reason without a desire, but presumably even a realist would agree that that is false in the case where you are ignorant of the facts about your interests. Clearly, no one would want to say that unperceived interests motivate. It is only an acknowledged interest which could conceivably cause a desire. So to generate

---

[43] Grice, 'Motive and Reason', p. 175.

a difference with the realist, Grice must assume that the agent knows the facts; the formula which he attacks ought then to read, 'No accepted reason without a desire'.

We are now in a better position to assess Grice's claim which is, taking account of these various points and complications, that you can accept that something is in your interests without your will's being affected, without being motivated to act on your perception. I want to argue that there are two possible interpretations of this claim, on the first of which it is implausible, and on the second ineffective.

I earlier drew attention to the distinction between prima-facie desires and all-things-considered desires, and that distinction is the basis of the two interpretations I have just mentioned. I should add that Grice does not distinguish the interpretations, but I think it is necessary. On the one interpretation, Grice's claim comes to this, that you can accept that something is in your interests without even wanting to some extent, or prima facie, to go for it. On the other, you can accept that something is in your interests without wanting on balance to go for it. Now the first interpretation is implausible. Cases like those of the boy who does not acquire a desire to go on the river and the actor who does not want to quit the stage suggest that self-interest can be defeated by other considerations, but not that it never enters the picture at all. It just does not seem true to say that normal people can be left quite cold by (acknowledged) facts about their interests. That would be a kind of madness. But Grice's agents are not represented as insane. Their state of mind is supposed to be quite common-place.

On the other hand, if Grice's claim is that you can accept that something is in your interests without acquiring an all-in desire to act on the judgement, that is likely to be agreed to by so many as almost to be a truism. Probably only a psycho-logical egoist would reject it, and certainly a realist need not. Think of McDowell's argument that if you are unmoved by thoughts about your future, you must have a different view of what it is for a fact to bear on your future. Presumably he has in mind a case where you are totally unmoved by such thoughts, for there is nothing in his view which requires you *always* to act on considerations of your interests. After all, other considerations—moral considerations, for example—can prove more important. And if you sacrifice your interests for moral motives, it cannot follow that there is some flaw in your understanding of what it is for a fact to concern your future. So McDowell must mean merely that someone with an understanding of their interests is thereby motivated to some extent by its demands. But then he is not damaged by Grice's claim on its alternative interpretation.

But if Grice's argument leaves realism intact, is there any other way to demonstrate its falsehood? I think there is. The question which Grice focuses on, namely whether you can accept that something is in your interests without as a consequence coming to care about it, is actually a red herring in this context. For even if it is conceded that all normal people do care, to some extent, realism need not follow. An anti-realist explanation of why our interests should sway us is that if we were not at all motivated by considerations of our interests, we should not survive; it is therefore psychologically impossible for normal human beings to be entirely indifferent to what they see as in their interests. The connection between valuation and action which this, if true, establishes, is quite different from the connection which the realist argument postulates. For on the realist argument, the connection is logical; here it is psychological. There the motivation is supposed to come from mere knowledge of the truth of the valuation: it is an internal guarantee. Here it comes from the fact that the pressures of survival ensure that we care about what happens to us: it is provided by something external to the valuation.

It is worth mentioning that some theorists believe something similar about moral motivation, or at least about some moral motivation, saying that the pressures of survival ensure that we care about what happens to other people, or at least some other people. I am thinking of the argument made familiar from socio-biology that genes which code for altruistic behaviour are more likely to survive. In particular, it is said that those genes are more likely to survive which lead parents to care for their children, and lead siblings and, to a lesser extent, other kin to care for each other. This seems to me much less plausible. Any interesting argument for morality will not, I think, be based on biological guarantees, for we do not tend to think of immoral people as *abnormal.*

The upshot of all this is that the correct way to decide whether the realist thesis is true or false is to determine whether it is just a general fact about human beings that we are motivated by our interests, or whether our being motivated by prudential considerations is rather a matter of understanding the meaning of what it is for a fact to concern our future. Realism wants to deny that there is any emotional contribution, even a universal emotional contribution, to our acting on prudential judgements. It wants to claim, to use an expression of Nagel's, that there are 'rational requirements on action',[44] and that recognition of the truth of a prudential judgement is enough to supply motivation. The other view is that the prudential judgement gives me a reason to act if I am a normal human being with the normal favourable attitudes towards my long-term interests. Now I argued against the interpretation of Grice's claim according to which he portrays as not unusual what would be a kind of insanity, namely if you suffered from a complete splitting off of acknowledged interest from desire. But although impossible in the normal course of events, the phenomenon is not literally unimaginable—any more than insanity is—and that suggests that realism is false. In the sort of case that McDowell describes, absence of motivation is better ascribed to psychological abnormality than to a different cognition. So whereas Grice is wrong to suggest that judgements about our interests need not normally sway us, realism is wrong about the reason why they do. The reason is because we are 'excited' by them; to borrow a term from Hutcheson.

One matter I have not discussed in this section is whether, if you judge *unconditionally* that it would be best for you to pursue your interests, your desires must fall in and comply. Realism must answer affirmatively. For if it is in the nature of a prudential judgement that it motivates, then the only thing that can impede action is an overriding consideration. If there is no overriding consideration, a conforming action must follow. But I have argued that realism is wrong and the

---

[44] Nagel, *The Possibility of Altruism,* p. 3.

judgement is not itself a motivation. The motivation comes from outside and depends on an additional psychological element. So even if there is no overriding consideration, you still have to want to do what you think best if action is to be the upshot. In the normal course of events you *will* want that, and it is no accident that you should, for dispassionate valuations are more likely to be geared to survival than desires unconstrained by reason. However, in Ch. V. 4 I say that the distorting effect of ideology can interfere with normal psychological processes, the consequence being that desires formed under the influence of ideology can resist an outright negative valuation and motivate in defiance of it. So Marxists should not defend the view that workers who are led by an objective assessment of their situation to judge that the overthrow of capitalism would unconditionally be best for them will necessarily be propelled in the direction of revolutionary activities.

5. FACTS AND INTERESTS

At the beginning of this chapter I said that I would defend two theses congenial to Marxism, namely that there is a fact of the matter about interests, and that interests are not want-based. The defence of the first of these will be the task of this section.

The first thing to see is that there is a concealed bonus in the anti-realist argument of the previous section, that a judgement about what is good for you is not enough, in itself, to generate desire. For if, as I argued, valuations are not logically guaranteed to motivate, that defeats the traditional argument for the conclusion that they do not state facts.

Let me explain what I mean. One of the theses of the doctrine I called 'subjectivism' is that prudential valuations are not factual. Supporting this claim are two Humean premisses. The first is that evaluative judgements have built into them a kind of magnetic force in that they move those who hold them to act on them. Why exactly this should be receives different answers from different philosophers. For instance, some claim that value-judgements express attitudes, others that they entail imperatives. But what unites all those who accept the first premiss is a theory about the essential practicality of value-judgements. The second premiss is that no belief could ever have a connection of that sort with the will: the facts on their own have no motivational force, but only motivate in combination with something like desires. It follows from the conjunction of these—the practical nature of evaluations and the 'inactivity' or detachment from action of beliefs—that prudential valuations cannot express beliefs—that is, that they cannot be assessed for truth and falsity. This is a non-cognitivist theory of value-judgements.

I agree with the second Humean premiss, that beliefs alone never provide a motive for action. But it was the upshot of the last section that prudential valuations have no necessary connection with the will either, and only move the agent in combination with an additional affective element. But if judgements about interests are not inherently practical, then they could express beliefs and the subjectivist thesis that that is impossible is wrong.

But do they express beliefs? Are there facts about interests? If interests were the same as biological needs, the answer to this would be straightforward. I think everyone will agree that there are facts about such needs, the idea of biological need being connected with the idea of the proper or healthy functioning of an organism. But there is no direct road from biological needs to interests for, on a proper understanding of the matter, biology only furnishes information about what is good for genes, and while what is good for my genes will usually be good for me, there can be no guarantee that they will always coincide. Lawrie Reznek has some nice examples of how they may come apart. He points out, for instance, that there are certain traits of organisms which are explained not by their propensity to enhance the survival chances of the individual, but by their propensity to enhance the survival chances of other individuals which share genetic material with it. The warning call given by certain squirrels, for instance, makes the caller conspicuous to predators, and therefore impairs *its* chances of survival. However, it enhances the survival chances of its *kin*, and the trait is therefore selected.[45] In short: interests cannot have their source in nature's often

---

[45] Reznek, *The Nature of Disease*, p. 102.

brutal plans for us. One of Fay Weldon's characters makes this point unanswerably, saying, 'it's natural to be dead'.[46]

But even if there is no direct road from biological needs to interests, the concept of biological need is still instructive. For the idea of proper or healthy functioning is a large part of the concept of 'interest' too, as is evident from the fact that it would be very odd to express a whimsical view about what is in someone's interests. The difference between biological needs and interests is just that when we know what your interests are, we know what it is for you to function effectively as a person, not what it is for you to function effectively as a biological organism. And the consequence is that we must look to psychology, not biology, for our knowledge of the facts relevant to interests. For instance, psychology may tell you that it will only bring you distress if you persist in trying to follow in an ambitious father's footsteps; or in obsessively pursuing wealth; or if you are committed to a life of duplicity with its attendant costs of hypocrisy and lack of spontaneity. Of course, there is more controversy about what psychological theory is true than about biological theories, but those who deny that there are facts about interests do not usually rest their case on the claim that psychology is unable to yield objective truths. Usually they accept that psychology can provide factual truths and think merely to deny that anything evaluative could follow from them. But I have argued that this denial rests on a misconception of the nature of evaluations. In particular, evaluations do not differ from the truths furnished by psychology in being necessarily practical. And once that obstacle to reducing judgements about interests to judgements about what way of life would suit or frustrate a person is gone, the only remaining task is to defend the analysis against alternative reductions. Its attractions will be explained in Ch. III. 7.

I suggest, then, that there are facts about what is in an individual's interests, that we should look for them in what causes that person to function effectively, and that a true psychological theory will uncover those causes. I think that Marx, however, took an extra step and held not merely that

<hr />

[46] Weldon, *Praxis*, p. 146.

what is good for a person is a factual matter but also that the good life is the same for everyone. This is an extra step, for nothing I have said so far implies that there could not be many ways to lead a worthwhile life, that each of us could not have entirely different sets of interests and flourish in different ways. In other words, there is nothing in the notion of objective interests which requires interests to be universally shared. I think Marx believed that there are universal human interests and that a certain, specific kind of life is good for all of us because he believed there is a universal human nature. It is fashionable to think that Marxism carries no commitment to such quaint ideas, but I do not see how else to make sense of much of Marx's thought. It is true that Marx frequently derided ahistorical conceptions of human nature, which confuse the contingent or impermanent characteristics of human beings in particular societies and at particular times with their essential characteristics, and which have an obvious tendency to shore up established political institutions. Bentham, for instance, is accused by Marx of taking 'the modern shopkeeper, especially the English shopkeeper, as the normal man. Whatever is useful to this queer, normal man, and to his world, is absolutely useful. This yard-measure, then, he applies to past, present, and future.'[47] Against such local and fossilized conceptions, Marx insisted that human beings transform themselves as they transform the material means of satisfying their wants. But what underlies that activity is an unchanging and uniquely human capacity, according to Marx, namely the capacity for free, conscious, and diverse productive activity. 'We see', Marx says, 'how the history of *industry* and the established *objective* existence of industry are the *open* book of *man's essential powers*, the perceptibly existing human *psychology*.'[48] Capitalism he saw as dehumanizing precisely to the extent that it inhibits the fullest exercise of that capacity. Under a system of private ownership of the means of production, labour is detested; it is a torture. The workers are in thrall to their products, their own petrified creations. The division of labour confines them to particular, exclusive

---

[47] *Capital*, i. 571, n.2.
[48] *Economic and Philosophic Manuscripts*, p. 302.

spheres of activity, which are forced upon them and from which there is no escape. They are mere fragments of human beings, tied to specialized, repetitive operations, at the expense of a whole world of productive capacities and inclinations. By contrast, under communism, circumstances will allow 'all-round activity' and 'the full development of all our potentialities'.[49] Communist society is 'the only society in which the genuine and free development of individuals ceases to be a mere phrase'.[50]

Marx himself tended to talk about human needs rather than human interests, and it is possible to use that vocabulary, just so long as one is careful to avoid identifying human needs with something like biological or subsistence needs. That would be wrong, not only for the reason I gave earlier, that biology is not essentially concerned with individuals, but also because it distorts Marx's thought on the matter. Wiggins is someone who is apparently guilty of this misidentification, for he seems to think that human needs for Marx were 'basic' needs, the 'thin set of universal needs that *nature* will underwrite'.[51] To some extent this misconception is caused by Marx's use of the concepts of 'natural' and 'human' interchangeably, which misleads if 'natural' is taken in the usual, biological sense. But Marx's concept of the natural is not biological. It is tied up with his beliefs about what way of life suits human beings. It is tied up, in other words, with his belief that psychological integration requires the 'absolute working-out of [our] creative potentialities'.[52] Indeed, so far from identifying the natural with the biologically basic, Marx calls 'unnatural' the 'simplicity of the *poor* and crude man who has few needs and who has not only failed to go beyond private property, but has not even reached it'.[53] The impression of paradox here should no longer surprise.

I do not believe there is anything to object to in Marx's extra step, the claim that we would all benefit from living a certain kind of life. Nothing in the notion of discoverable interests

[49] *The German Ideology*, p. 255.
[50] Ibid. 439.
[51] Wiggins, 'Claims of Need', p. 20, n. 22.
[52] *Grundrisse*, p. 488.
[53] *Economic and Philosophic Manuscripts*, p. 295.

implies that they are not universal. And while it is no doubt true that not all interests are shared, it is quite likely that some are, for it is quite likely that there are common elements in our psychologies—that is, that to some extent we share a psychological nature. Of course, Marx might have been quite wrong in thinking that it is self-realization which is the route to human fulfilment. But that is a different matter.

6. REASONS

In the last section I argued against one of the subjectivist doctrines, the one which says that what is good for people cannot be a matter of fact. In the next section, I shall argue against the other, the one which says that interests are want-based. But before I come to that I must say something brief about reasons. I said, when discussing Grice's theory, that he thinks that reasons have nothing to do with motivation, but that I think it impossible that someone might have a reason to act in a certain way and yet no tendency to act on it. I mean logically impossible, not merely psychologically impossible for a normal human being. That is because when you have a reason there is an available description under which your action makes sense for you, and that means citing both a relevant belief and a relevant desire. It is the desire, of course, which does the motivating. I follow Davidson here.[54]

My theory therefore differs from Grice's in two ways. The one difference, discussed in Ch. III. 4, is that he believes that prudential value-judgements need not, in the normal course of events, motivate at all, whereas I argued that they do normally motivate. The other difference is that he is committed both to a gap between valuations and reasons and to one between reasons and actions, while I have argued only for the former. (See Table 3.3 for a diagrammatic representation of the differences between my theory and Grice's.)

It is worth pointing out that if valuations are not inherently practical, as I argued in Ch. III. 4, it follows from what I have said here about the inherently practical and therefore dissimilar nature of reasons that what you think best to do and

---

[54] Davidson, 'Actions, Reasons and Causes', in *Essays on Actions and Events*, pp. 3–4.

TABLE 3.3

		Interests are want-independent	Interests are want-based	Wants are interest-based
Prudential judgements express beliefs	Perception of interests is contingently practical	Perception of interests does not in itself yield a reason	Favoured theory		True want theory
	Perception of interests is not practical	Perception of interests does in itself yield a reason	Grice's theory		
	Perception of interests is necessarily practical		Realism		
Prudential judgements express desires				Subjectivism	

what you have reason to do do not necessarily coincide. In other words, it is possible for you to act on a reason although you see no overall value in your act. It is your desire to do the unconditionally negatively valued act which is your reason for doing it. Weakness of will is probably the most accessible example of this phenomenon, for there is in the weakness case a ready explanation of how it happens, namely that the agent is acting on a desire which has a close connection with immediate sensory pleasure. It is easy to see why such a desire should have the excessive motivational strength it does. But it is not essential that there should be some prospect of immediate sensory gratifications. When I talked, in Ch. II. 5, about conscious belief against the weight of the evidence, I said that often a desire causes the irrational belief, but that I would show later that nothing so obviously powerful is essential. Acting on a reason—that is, acting intentionally—against an all-out value-judgement is similar to conscious belief in the teeth of the evidence in that the agent may once more not be propelled by anything highly dramatic. Again that is merely a promissory note and I shall come back to the point later, in Ch. V. 4.

What does the belief that reasons motivate imply? Bernard Williams thinks that it has more far-reaching consequences than it actually does. He distinguishes 'internal' from 'external' reasons. Roughly speaking, you have an internal reason to F, according to Williams, when your F-ing will serve some motive of yours. If you have an external reason to F, by contrast, the reason for you to F does not rest on any motive of yours and rational deliberation alone could lead you to want to F. Williams does not think there are any external reasons. He uses as an example James's story of Owen Wingrave, whose father thinks Owen has a reason to join the army because it is traditional in their family, although Owen hates everything about military life, and has no desire to join. Williams says that Owen's father's external reason statement, like all external reason statements, is false. As will be evident from what I said earlier about the connection between specifying a reason and referring to a desire, I agree. However, Williams does not merely deny that Owen has a reason to join the army. He also claims that Owen cannot be said to be unreasonable or irrational in failing to join. He seems to think it follows from the fact that a consideration which is outside your motivational set cannot be a reason for you, that it therefore cannot be unreasonable of you when you fail to act in the way you would be disposed to, had you the reason. He says:

> those who use [external reason statements] often seem . . . to be entertaining an optimistic internal reason claim. But sometimes the statement is indeed offered as standing definitely outside the agent's [subjective motivational set] and what he might derive from it in rational deliberation, and then there is, I suggest, a great unclarity about what is meant. Sometimes it is little more than that things would be better if the agent so acted. But the formulation in terms of reasons does have an effect, particularly in its suggestion that the agent is being irrational, and this suggestion, once the basis of an internal reason claim has been clearly laid aside, is bluff.[55]

I think Williams is wrong. While it is true that only what serves some motive of yours can give you a reason to act, it does not follow that only what serves your motives is reasonable or rational for you. 'Reason' is an explanatory notion. Judgements as to what is reasonable or rational are, by contrast, value-judgements. Williams's argument would succeed if *F*-ing could only be said to be the most reasonable action for you if you believed it to be the most reasonable action for you. However, Williams does not try to show that and so his identification of what is rational for the agent with what the agent is motivated to do is suspect.

Jonathan Lear, in his paper 'Moral Objectivity', argues that there is a kind of reason which is neither external nor internal but 'objective', and that you can have an objective reason to *F* when you have neither an internal nor an external reason to *F*. As an example he describes a man who because of a shameful incident has decided to commit suicide, but of whom it is true that, if he did not commit suicide, then at some later time he would find life worth living. This man does not have an internal reason not to kill himself, for he lacks the motivation to go on living. And although he recognizes that at some later time he would find life worth living, this recognition has no force in the presence of his powerful present desire to avoid

---

[55] Williams, 'Internal and External Reasons', p. 26.

shame at all costs. So, since rational deliberation cannot change his mind, he does not have an external reason either. But Lear says he has an objective reason not to kill himself for he has a reason to 'flourish'. This objective reason exists despite the fact that he is not and cannot be motivated to flourish.[56] As I have said, I believe that all reasons are internal because reasons explain actions. I should therefore deny that this man has an objective reason not to kill himself, for the 'reason' *ex hypothesi* does not connect with his motivations. To some extent this is a terminological matter because of course I think it would be better for the man if he did not kill himself; it is just that I do not think the way to explain why his motivations are deficient has anything to do with reasons.

To sum up: actions are explained by reasons but the reasons which explain actions are not necessarily rational ones. This is so first because my reason for my action need not match my unconditional value-judgement, and second because my motivations may be unreasonable or irrational.

7. A WANT-INDEPENDENT CONCEPTION OF INTERESTS

The theory I called 'subjectivism' consists in twin doctrines. I have already discussed the one which asserts that there is no fact of the matter about interests. It is false if my earlier argument in Ch. III. 5 is right. The first subjectivist doctrine is subjectivist about prudential judgements. The other subjectivist doctrine—the one I want to discuss now—has a subjective conception of interests. Where the first asserts that judgements about interests express desires, the second holds, roughly, that the way to realize interests is to fulfil desires. I say 'roughly' because there is that complication I talked about, which has to do with the fact that any theory which locates value in the fulfilment of desires must confine itself to desires which are not based on false belief. However I shall not keep mentioning that refinement, and shall assume in what follows that the desires whose fulfilment the theory values have survived exposure to all the relevant facts.

[56] Lear, 'Moral Objectivity', pp. 140–4.

The subjective or want-based conception is really the ortho-doxy. Indeed it is a view whose plausibility is almost un-examined. It is held in one form or another not only by most philosophers but also by politicians, social scientists, and economists. Here, for instance, is R. M. Hare speaking for the orthodoxy in *Freedom and Reason*: 'To have an interest is, crudely speaking, for there to be something which one wants, or is likely in the future to want, or which is (or is likely to be) a means necessary or sufficient for the attainment of something which one wants (or is likely to want).'[57] Again, one kind of utilitarian holds to another version of the orthodoxy, believing that nothing has value except as it contributes to want-satisfaction. And for a final example, there are those modern economists who look for what makes you better off in what you choose or prefer. One way they achieve this is by definition, so that the satisfaction of your preferences just has, vacuously, to be in your interests. But there is also another way in which the connection between preferences and interests can be assured and that is on the empirical assumption that people's choices are always motivated by self-interest.

Some will object to the way I have set up the issue, as involving a contest between a want-based and a want-independent conception of interests, that it altogether misses out a third possibility, which is that what is in our interests is the obtaining of pleasant states of mind. Although different from the want-based conception, this objector may continue—for we desire many things other than pleasant feelings—this hedonistic theory has more in common with the want-based than the want-independent conception of interests, as can be gathered from the fact that utilitarianism can take either form, aiming to maximize either want-satisfaction or pleasant feelings.

It is true that I narrowed down the topic when I set up the issue but there was a reason for my omission. The reason is that I do not think the hedonistic theory even gets off the ground. One familiar example which shows this is that of the man who gets pleasure from thoughts of his wife's fidelity, although in fact he is betrayed. He is harmed by the infidelity

---

[57] Hare, *Freedom and Reason*, p. 122.

he does not know about because what is in our interests is that what is good for us should actually come about. If this were not the case we would have reason to be hypnotized or drugged into believing that our interests have been promoted. Consequently the man whose wife is unfaithful suffers damage to his interests, although he experiences no unpleasant mental state. What is in his interests is that his wife should be faithful, not that he should believe her so. Again, his interests are harmed when the person he believes his friend belittles him behind his back. Since you need not know that your interests have been frustrated for them to be frustrated, it follows that interests cannot be defined in terms of subjective states.

'But', it might be asked, 'is it not the case that we feel pleasure when what is in our interests comes about?' I think that what needs to be said here is that even if the answer to that question is 'yes', the hedonistic theory reverses the direction of explanation. It is because these things make us better off that, when they come about, we feel pleasure, if we do indeed feel pleasure. It is impossible that it should be the other way round, that they should make us better off because they give pleasure, for that would make the reason for the pleasure obscure. Nagel makes an analogous point about undergoing misfortune, which is the counterpart of being well off. He says:

Someone who holds that all goods and evils must be temporally assignable states of the person may . . . try to bring difficult cases into line by pointing to the pleasure or pain that more complicated goods and evils cause. Loss, betrayal, deception, and ridicule are on this view bad because people suffer when they learn of them. But it should be asked how our ideas of human value would have to be constituted to accommodate these cases directly instead. One advantage of such an account might be that it enables us to explain *why* the discovery of these misfortunes causes suffering—in a way that makes it reasonable. For the natural view is that the discovery of betrayal makes us unhappy because it is bad to be betrayed—not that betrayal is bad because its discovery makes us unhappy.[58]

I conclude therefore that interests ought to be tied to the coming about of states of the world, not states of mind. It

[58] Nagel, 'Death', p. 5.

follows that the want-based is more plausible than the hedonistic conception of interests, for at least it does tie interests to the coming about of states of affairs. But is it right that those states of affairs must be wanted states of affairs? Marxism resists that identification, and I shall argue in what follows that it does so rightly: the happening of states of affairs we desire does not necessarily make us better off.

I want to begin by setting aside what might seem to be a tangential bit of support for the want-based conception of interests and after that I shall tackle the issue more directly. It is well known that Plato wanted to define the good life in terms of the moral life, a definition which implies that we are made better off by living a moral rather than an immoral life. But that could only be plausible if interests had nothing to do with what people actually want, for clearly the moral life does not satisfy the wicked person's here-and-now desires. Plato's view is that, want it or not, a virtuous life is in our interests. Now someone unsympathetic to the connection which Plato makes between morality and interests might think that the answer is to avoid divorcing interests from wants. This seems to be the assumption behind an argument of Joel Feinberg's. He wants to protect the claims of virtue against the encroachments of self-interest. He writes: 'there is no necessity that excellence and happiness always coincide, no impossibility that morally inferior persons can be happy, and excellent persons miserable.'[59] Later he adds, 'Self-interest . . . isn't everything. It is no aid to clarity to insist that everything that is good *in* a person must be good *for* the person . . . The contented moral defective . . . is both evil and well-off, and his evil character does not detract from his well-offness.'[60] Excellence is always a good thing, he concludes, but it is only if we desire excellence that it is in our interest to be excellent.[61] Interests, in other words, must be associated with what people actually want.

The problem with this account is in the paradoxical combination of claims that although excellent persons can be miserable, if they desire to be excellent excellence is in their

---

[59] Feinberg, 'Harm and Self-Interest', p. 48.
[60] Ibid. 49–50.
[61] Ibid. 48.

interests. The paradox comes from thinking that where Plato went wrong was in rejecting a want-based theory of interests. Fortunately there is a better way of resisting the usurpation of virtue, its swallowing up by self-interest. The real reason why a virtuous life need not be in the interests of the person who has no desire to be virtuous is because virtue can require us to sacrifice our interests for those of other people. I say more about this below. For the moment it is only necessary to see that the absence of a desire to be virtuous is actually irrelevant to the explanation of the non-coincidence of virtue and self-interest, and the presence of such a desire could not restore the coincidence. In other words, the autonomy of virtue is a red herring in this context, and fails to bear on the question of the proper understanding of interests.

Why should it be thought that what is good for you is the coming about of states of the world that you want? It is actually quite hard to find any arguments, probably because the view is so much taken on trust. One line of thought which might perhaps support it is the naturalistic one that we want what is good for us, and we avoid what is not, and it is no accident that we should, for if we continually desired self-destructive things we should not survive long. In other words, the pressures of survival ensure that the objects of our desires are in our interests. But I do not think this argument succeeds. For one thing, not all our desires are of the sort to be selected for, for not all are coded for in the genes. Consequently they are not all connected in the postulated way with prospects of survival. If they were, we could expect cigarette smokers not merely to die earlier but to die out altogether. A second difficulty with the naturalistic line of thought is that even if, for the sake of argument, we concentrate only on desires which do have a connection with survival, there is in any case no guarantee that what we desire will turn out to be good for *us*, or in *our* interests. This is for a reason I gave in Ch. III. 5: the unit of selection is not the individual, but the gene, and there may be all sorts of desires which improve the survival prospects of the gene, which are 'in the interests of' the gene, but whose satisfaction leaves the individual worse off.

If arguments for the want-based conception are hard to find, are there any arguments against it? One thing which

suggests that it is wrong is the existence in people of moral
motives. I have already said that I think Plato was wrong in
thinking that the virtuous person is necessarily better off.
Feinberg takes this to show that what makes you better off is
getting what you want. But actually it demonstrates the
opposite. Virtuous agents do get what they want, for they want
what is right, but their interests are not necessarily served by
the fulfilment of their desires. The truth is that, want it or not,
a virtuous life is not guaranteed to be in our interests. The
most straightforward way to show this is to point out that
people may, acting out of principle, make sacrifices. It is well
known that Kant thought acting from principle the only form
of moral motivation. He says of a man who takes pleasure in
'spreading happiness' around him that his action has no true
moral worth. But if such a man, he says, finding himself all of a
sudden 'no longer moved by any inclination', his sympathy
extinguished, still 'tears himself out of this deadly insensibility
and does the action without any inclination for the sake of
duty alone; then for the first time his action has genuine moral
worth'.[62] There are few who would agree with Kant that the
agent who cares about the welfare of others, out of love, or
friendship, or sympathy, does not act from a moral motive.
But, unattractive as he is, Kant's dutiful man proves my point
quite straightforwardly. Suppose, in the extreme case, that he
gives up his life for others. It is commonsensical to say that his
interests are not served; yet to give up his life is what he wants.
It is true that he acts unsolicited by inclination. But all that can
mean is that there is nothing personally appealing to him in
the act. Since he is motivated by the consideration that self-
sacrifice is right, he wants on balance to sacrifice himself, and
that is enough to make him a counter-example to the thesis
that interests are want-based. On the other hand, he is not
acting out of love or some similar emotion and that is what
makes him quite a straightforward counter-example, for it is a
possible view that if you make a sacrifice out of love your
interests are served. But that is not in the least plausible when
said about the dutiful man.

   In fact I think that even a sacrifice out of love is a sacrifice of

---

[62] Kant, *The Groundwork of the Metaphysic of Morals*, p. 64.

interests, although that is not as straightforward to show, nor is showing it strictly necessary, the dutiful agent being enough of a counter-example to a want-based theory of interests. Still, it is worth considering the view which distinguishes an agent moved by love or some similar emotion from an agent moved by duty, and says their motives have an impact on their interests. This view says that when you have an intrinsic desire for someone else's happiness, when you want that person to be happy not as a means to your own happiness but as an end in itself, then you have an *interest* in that person's interests. Feinberg argues for this in the same paper I have already mentioned. He says that to desire someone else's good as an end in itself is to 'gain or lose directly depending on the condition of the other person'.[63] The trouble with this is that it implies, counter-intuitively, that *your* well-being can be improved or diminished by events you neither know about nor desire for yourself. It is true that I gave examples earlier, when arguing against the hedonistic conception of interests, of cases in which the fulfilment or frustration of your desires affects your interests independently of your knowledge. But in those cases the desires were desires for yourself. By contrast, Feinberg's account implies that your interests can be affected by events you not only do not know about but also do not desire for yourself. And, as Derek Parfit says, of a case where I meet a stranger and out of sympathy acquire a strong desire for her to succeed, 'It is not plausible to claim that if, unknown to me, this stranger does later succeed, this is good for me . . . if desires are not about my own life, and I never know they are fulfilled, we may find it hard to believe that the fulfilment of these desires will be good for me.'[64] I think Parfit is right, and that your interests must be a matter of your *own* good. It follows that neither the interests of the dutiful agent nor those of the agent who makes a sacrifice out of love are served by the fulfilment of their desires.

But perhaps it will be objected that the fulfilment of their desires is in the interests of *both* the agent who acts out of emotion and the dutiful agent, not for Feinberg's reason, but because individuals are incapable of any motivation which is

---

[63] Feinberg, 'Harm and Self-Interest', p. 56.
[64] Parfit, *Reasons and Persons*, p. 468.

not self-interested, the only thing that we all desire for its own sake being our own well-being. It is very hard to argue once and for all against such a view, that when we desire the well-being of others that is always as a means to our own. All you can do is point to examples of courage and sacrifice in which to postulate an underlying selfish motive makes little sense. Many sacrifices do not bring pleasure or happiness, and even when they do have repercussions of that kind, the pleasure or happiness need not be the reason for the sacrifice. It can be the other person's well-being which is aimed at, not the agent's, and when that is achieved, the agent's satisfaction is merely consequential.

I hope I have shown that the fulfilment of desires for other people's well-being can clash with an agent's interests. But that is not the end of the matter because a want-based theory need not be so ambitious as to deny that. A less ambitious theory might prefer to confine its claims to desires about the agent's own life, on the assumption that it must at any rate be the case that the fulfilment of my desires for myself makes me better off.

But even that is not necessarily true. For one thing, there are the aberrant desires with which psychology deals—self-destructive desires, mad desires, desires for meaningless and ritualistic activities. The examples could be multiplied, the common denominator here being pathology as it is not with the desires of the virtuous person. (Of course, there are those who would say that there is also pathology in acting on a moral impulse, Nietzsche being a notable example. One answer to Nietzsche is Plato's, that the virtuous person is better off, but I have argued against that claim. I think the right reply to Nietzsche is rather that it is not irrational to choose the virtuous option.) Then there are the more mundane temptations of everyday life. Smoking is an obvious example. If we were to say that you are made worse off when your crazy or unhealthy desires are not fulfilled, then we should be muddling the difference between interests and desires. For lack of what is in our interests injures us. Interests therefore have an inbuilt connection with well-being and we must look outside ourselves, to the truths furnished by psychology, to discover what it is that will make our lives go well.

By contrast, desires have no such connection, as Richard
Wollheim points out. To lack what you desire is not necessarily
to ail, and to be in a position to ascribe a desire to someone, all
we have to know about is that person's mental state.[65] But is it
not the case that the mental state of someone whose desire is
unsatisfied is *painful*, which would make for the connection
with well-being just denied? One reply to this is that not all
unsatisfied desire involves pain. Another reply, which is
Wollheim's, is that it may be better to have a desire unsatisfied
than not to have desired at all.[66] Powering the lives of many
exceptional individuals are enormous visions which are
impossible to fulfil. This difference between interests and
desires, that ascription of the former but not the latter
requires knowledge of more than people's mental states, is
reflected in a formal difference. If x is in my interests, then
anything identical with x is also in my interests. But if I desire
x, I do not necessarily desire everything identical with x,
'desire' being an intentional verb.[67]

Well, is it not then the case that when people act on desires
which risk their health they are victims of some false belief?
Not at all. Jonathan Lear gives an example of an alcoholic who,
once he has become drunk, wants only to continue drinking.
How likely is it that he is acting on a false belief—for instance,
that drinking leads to longevity? Mostly such people are not
ignorant of anything an outsider knows and the facts have
little relevance to how they act.[68] But perhaps it will be
objected that there *is* false belief behind desires whose fulfilment makes people worse off, for people who have such
desires have a false theory about what is good for them and
that explains why they want what they do. But once a want-
based conception of interests retreats this far, there is no
longer anything to distinguish it from its opponent. Having
conceded that there can be such a thing as evaluative information, it has conceded everything to the want-independent
conception whose main claim, after all, is that value has just

[65] Wollheim, 'Needs, Desires and Moral Turpitude', pp. 175–6.
[66] Ibid. 175.
[67] Wiggins makes this point about needs and desires. See 'Claims of Need', p. 6.
[68] Lear, 'Moral Objectivity', pp. 152–3.

that kind of independent basis, in a theory of objective interests.

There is one last compromise I must consider which is whether we could not perhaps isolate some of our desires and say that those, at any rate, are the clue to what is in our interests. I shall consider some plausible-looking candidates to play that role, say why they fail, and then give a general reason why the idea of fixing on or isolating a sub-class of desires cannot salvage even the last remnants of a want-based theory of interests.

Someone impressed by the fact that sometimes the operation of an irresistible desire is essential to survival might hypothesize that it must be good for you when the desires by which you cannot but be moved are satisfied. But in fact there are desires which move us willy-nilly which we could lose without suffering any harm. It is enough to consider neurotically compulsive actions to see that interests cannot be connected with desires which move us involuntarily in the way the hypothesis suggests. A person may be unable to resist the desire to indulge in some ritualistic activity; but it certainly does not follow that we are obliged to take the desire at face value and think its satisfaction worthwhile. So there is not necessarily value in the satisfaction of a desire by which you are irresistibly moved. What is more, something can be in your interests even though you fail to be moved by it. An example is the anorexic's refusal to eat.

A second hypothesis might be that it is only desires by which *no one* fails to be moved whose satisfaction is connected with interests. This is not open to the counter-example of compulsive neuroses, for only some people are beset by those, but it is problematic in other ways. First of all, it is problematic because it cannot do justice to the fact that we have an idea of interests relative to individuals and to social groups. In the individual case, we need only think of someone with a special handicap. Clearly, the amelioration of the handicapped's handicaps is in their interests, whether others are moved by the desire for that amelioration or not. But on the hypothesis about interests which we are considering, on which only desires by which no one fails to be moved are connected with interests, amelioration of their handicaps would not be in the interests of the handicapped for not everyone cares about their situation. The same point can be made with respect to groups. Stuart Hampshire talks of social customs and habits which differ from group to group but whose observance is still tremendously important for their members—such things as sexual practices and prohibitions, duties to do with the dead, and obligations to friends and family.[69] Clearly, what the members of one group take as specially significant may not move the members of another but it would be wrong to think that their concerns, being idiosyncratic, have nothing to do with their interests. Naturally I do not mean to exclude the possibility that some benefits benefit all of us, in virtue of our nature; but I do deny that these are the only benefits there are. This is another difference between interests and biological needs, that biological needs are shared by all members of the species, whereas interests are not confined in that way and need not be common. The concept allows for individual variations.

So one reason why interests cannot be connected with desires by which no one fails to be moved is that what is in the interests of one individual or the members of one group need not move another individual or the members of another group. A second reason is that there is not necessarily value in the satisfaction of desires which move everyone. Everyone may be conditioned, after all, a possibility which is quite relevant in this context, given that Marxists are so likely to exploit it.

Someone encouraged by some remarks of Richard Brandt might argue that the correct criterion is inextinguishability rather than irresistibility. Conditioned desires, this person might say, can be reversed by counter-conditioning and there is therefore no reason to value their satisfaction. It is only unextinguishable desires, or desires we cannot help experiencing, whose satisfaction is in our interests. I say that this criterion is inspired by Brandt for he says that if a desire fails to be extinguished (after being confronted with relevant information) then it is not irrational: 'a desire . . . is rational if it has been influenced by facts and logic as much as possible. Un-

---

[69] Hampshire, 'Morality and Convention', p. 153.

extinguishable desires meet this condition.'[70] But, his excessive optimism about the power of facts and logic to extinguish irrational desires apart, it is not true even of universally experienced, unextinguishable desires that their satisfaction is guaranteed to be a good thing. For if any desires are un-extinguishable they will be desires with which we are 'wired up'. But, as I said before, the unit of selection is the gene, not the individual. Consequently it is possible that we will have inherited desires whose satisfaction, although it maximizes the chances of gene survival, is not good for us.

The more general point is that no class of desires could be connected as such with interests. Even if it were in a person's interests to have a universal or near-universal or any other central kind of desire satisfied, the explanation could never be 'because it is that kind of desire', but only 'because such desires are in fact connected with objective interests determined independently of desires'. Because, for instance, it is thought that universal desires have something to do with our healthy functioning. If there were not that explanation, the reason for fixing on this one class of desires would be a mystery. Another way of putting this is to say that the fact that a desire has certain characteristics could never make its satisfaction valu-able. All it could do is be a symptom of value, or indicate that there is value in the desire's satisfaction—but then the value itself would have an independent basis, in a theory of objec-tive interests. What is in your interests depends not on your desires, nor on any class of them, but on what is the good life for you. Marx, of course, had a particular vision of that, as promoting what he calls in the *Grundrisse* 'the absolute working-out of man's creative potentialities'.[71] But whether you agree with Marx or not, some or other vision of the good life—perhaps fulfilling the duties of your station, or living passionately, or submitting to God's will, or whatever—must inform the notion of interests.

I have now finished my argument against the want-based conception of interests and shall conclude this section with some observations about the way in which desire aims at

---

[70] Brandt, *A Theory of the Good and the Right*, p. 113.
[71] *Grundrisse*, p. 488.

something and how much that way is like the way in which belief aims at the truth.[72] I think there is an analogy here but its limits are quite precise. For one thing, it would be far too strong to think that it could be truth at which desire aims or that there could be such a thing as a literally false desire. On the other hand, someone might think that Anscombe's view, that the concept of wanting implies that you should see what you want under the aspect of some good, could be put by saying that desire aims at the good, although in fact what Anscombe means is too weak to make for any points of analogy with belief. Anscombe's view is that there is a conceptual connection between 'wanting' and 'good', that the object desired has to be thought desirable or worth having in some way. However for her '*bonum est multiplex*':[73] there are no limits on what may justifiably be thought good or desirable. The only way, for Anscombe, in which you can go wrong is in your belief that some object possesses the feature you think good. You cannot be wrong in thinking that feature good.[74] But this means that for Anscombe desire cannot really *aim* at the good, for it cannot *miss*. There is only a point to the aiming metaphor if desire itself can fall short of the good, if it is possible to say that what you want is not, objectively speaking, desirable. Consider the reason why we say belief aims at the truth: it is because beliefs can display a feature, falsity, which they ought not to. They can suffer a defect. So if there were an analogy between belief and desire, if desire aimed at the good in an analogous way to the way in which belief aims at the truth, there would have to be a way in which desires could suffer a defect. Now on my view, by contrast with Anscombe's, there is such a way, for we have seen that the satisfaction of our desires may not be good for us. And if we add that we ought at least prima facie to want what is in our interests—and one use of 'rational' is just in terms of interests—we see that the aiming metaphor is a legitimate way of expressing the truth in the want-independent conception of interests. Desires can have a feature they ought not to have. The target in the case of desire is our well-being, and to the extent that our

---

[72] See Williams, 'Deciding to Believe', p. 136.
[73] Anscombe, *Intention*, p. 75.
[74] Ibid. 76–7.

desires are out of touch with that, they go wrong. There is a norm in the case of desire, just as there is with belief.

It may be objected as follows: I have said that there is no pathology in the desires of virtuous individuals and that it is not necessarily irrational to make sacrifices which diminish your well-being, but that is incompatible with the idea that it is a defect in a desire that its fulfilment should make the agent worse off. I have two replies to this. One is that I was talking about desires for oneself. It is a defect in these desires that their fulfilment should make you worse off. The desires of the virtuous person are about other people's lives and if they aim at something, it will be a different target. The second reply is that failing to do the agent any good is only one way in which a desire can go wrong and that defect might be tolerated, indeed even urged, on account of moral considerations which override it.

But perhaps it will be objected now that the reason we think beliefs ought to be true is because to believe some proposition *p* is to believe it true. Consequently you cannot straightforwardly, or without self-deception, believe what you think false or likely to be false. It follows, this objector continues, that if the analogy were right, if desires aimed at well-being in the way in which beliefs aim at the truth, then you could not straightforwardly desire something unless you believed it worthwhile. But you *can* straightforwardly desire what you believe unworthwhile. For instance, you can crave to eat something bizarre. So in what sense is there a norm for desire?

One way out of this for me would be to deny that you can desire what you unconditionally believe bad for you. But in fact, as I have said, I accept that desires can fail to fall in with valuations. I think the right rejoinder is rather to question the assumption that you cannot believe *p* recognizing that the evidence is against it. In fact I argue in Chapter V that beliefs can resist the evidence that they are false even in the absence of any motivational impetus. At most there is a difference of degree here, desires possibly being more likely to survive a negative valuation than beliefs to survive acknowledged contrary evidence.

I suppose the objection might be refined, and it might be said that you cannot, except compulsively, believe what you think false, while you can without compulsion desire what you believe bad for you. But this more subtle objection gets its force from the implicit suggestion of obsession or madness in the belief which survives contrary evidence. I shall be arguing, however, that there can be insensitivity to evidence without madness, and then the difference between belief and desire will again seem less clear.

However, there is this difference, that even if both belief and desire aim at something, what belief aims at is not dependent on facts about human beings, whereas what desire aims at is. As far as the relation of thought to reality is concerned, we think of knowledge as of a reality which exists independently of our thoughts about it, and which may indeed transcend them in the sense that what there is may be out of the grasp of creatures like us. This is what Williams calls the 'absolute conception' of reality.[75] By contrast, what I have said about value suggests that it depends entirely on facts about the psychological nature of human beings. Wiggins is right to say that the category of value is anthropocentric, that it is relative to human concerns.[76] This does not imply that what is of value must be recognized by us, but only that it can be recognized by us. It also implies that the facts about value suggest no answer, and can suggest no answer, to the question, 'What ought a rational creature, any rational creature, to want?' After all, other rational creatures may have entirely different characters from ours. The facts about value tell us what *we* ought to want, but they are no less facts on account of that restriction.

*

If we now take all the arguments of this chapter together, the main conclusions to emerge are these.

1. The first of the two assertions to which I originally said a Marxist was committed by the notion of proletarian false consciousness, namely that there is a fact of the matter about interests, is sound.
2. The want-based conception of interests cannot be right for interests articulate not with what is wanted but with the

---

[75] Williams, *Descartes: The Project of Pure Enquiry*, pp. 64–5.
[76] Wiggins, 'Truth, Invention, and the Meaning of Life', p. 349.

good life. It follows that the second of the Marxist assertions is also sound, namely that what is good for people
does not depend on what they want.
3. The realist version of Marxism, on which bare knowledge
of the facts about interests elicits desire, is false.
4. The true want version is also false, on which to be wrong
about what is in your interests is to be wrong about your
desires.

The upshot is that it is a plausible Marxism which says that
there are facts about interests, that the facts are facts about the
good life, and that to accept the facts is not automatically to
acquire matching motivation. Furthermore, this version of
Marxism is plausible not only on account of making good
philosophical sense, in being consonant with what I have
argued are the correct conclusions about interests. It also
makes good exegetical sense, for it gels nicely with some other
aspects of Marxist thought. Marxists say that people can have
false beliefs about what is good for them, that they can be
seduced by the wrong kinds of goal. If we ask the obvious
question, which is why they should make such unprofitable
choices, the Marxist answer is that economic and social
arrangements make for a feeling of naturalness or common-
placeness about some goals and aspirations, and not others.
They are in the air we breathe. Like the categories of
bourgeois economic theory which are also extruded by the
economic system, they have 'acquired the stability of natural,
self-understood forms of social life'.[77] But the naturalness of
some motivations, and the invisibility of their opposites, is
really the other side of the coin from the independence of
desires from valuations. For if some aspirations have a kind of
social accreditation, it is easy to understand why they should
resist a negative valuation as the version of Marxism I have
argued for claims they can. After all, to be told, or to read in
Marx, that they are inappropriate is not to have their salience
or naturalness dispelled. Social and economic arrangements
would have to change for that. Consequently people who
accept Marx's valuation are not guaranteed a transformation

---

[77] *Capital*, i. 80.

in their motivations; the motivation which matches the valuation will continue to seem maverick. Another way of putting this is to say that people who read Marx and come to believe that their goals are inappropriate do not acquire their belief from an experience. The result is that they accept the valuation as an outsider would. In effect, they stand aside and take an overseer's view of their own interests and the thoroughly Marxist explanation is: years and years of social conditioning. No doubt a Marxist would want to add that in a different society people will come to want what is of value, but that is not incompatible with the truth of the view that valuations are not guaranteed to motivate. For the transformation in desires requires something extra, a change in the world, the abolition of private ownership of the means of production, not just a different cognition. This is all very brief, and I shall say more later about the independence of desires from valuations and how much irrationality there is when they come apart (see Ch. V. 4). But I wanted to make the point here that the possibility of their autonomy fits well with Marxist claims about social conditioning.

It is worth mentioning that we should expect to find the same autonomy of desires and motivations in women if they too have been thoroughly conditioned contrary to their interests, and the syndrome is indeed described in feminist writing. Jean Grimshaw, for instance, mentions how 'Images of Women' criticism, which aims to show how images of women in the media and elsewhere oppress and undermine them, can fail to dislodge the appeal of these images even to avowedly feminist women, who nevertheless cannot help remaining committed to them 'in emotion and desire'.[78]

---

[78] Grimshaw, 'Autonomy and Identity in Feminist Thinking', p. 100.

IV
Rogue Desires

1. A HISTORY FOR DESIRES

In the last chapter I assumed that when Marxists describe those who, according to them, have inauthentic values, or false needs, or inappropriate desires, as suffering from false consciousness, the intention is to express a kind of scepticism about the value of what the victims of ideology pursue, and I argued that the underlying idea, that it can be objectively stated that what people want is not necessarily what is good for them, can be defended philosophically. But there is a second possible way of understanding these phrases and that is to suppose that the idea is to launch an attack on the causes of ideological desires. Marcuse, for instance, says not merely that 'false needs' 'perpetuate toil, aggressiveness, misery and injustice', but also that they are 'determined by external powers over which the individual has no control'.[1] I want to explore this second possibility now and investigate whether the history of a desire can be a defect in it, and in particular whether the history of ideological desires makes for a defect.

What answer, compatible with Marxism, is there to the question of how people might acquire ideological desires? Marxism implies that they are to be explained by the character of the relations of production and that they entrench those relations. Clearly, just the same question arises here as arose for the ideological rationalizations discussed earlier in this book, namely how are these two claims to be combined? How can the explanatory role of the relations of production be construed in a way which accommodates their being agreeably affected by the prevalent conservative values? I argued in Ch. I. 5 that the right answer to the question about the rationalizations is that they are believed because of their propensity to have a certain kind of effect on the economy,

[1] Marcuse, *One-Dimensional Man*, p. 5.

and I now want to extend that to ideological desires: it is because they suit or consolidate economic relations that they get a grip. The desires are explained by their effect on economic relations. But then, just as with the rationalizations, there will have to be some supplementary account of how it is that their useful effect explains their prevalence.

In the case of the rationalizations, the focus was on how those who benefit from their legitimating effect on the economy might come to believe them. That posed a problem because of a fact about belief, namely that beliefs aim to represent reality. Consequently there is a considerable degree of irrationality involved when beliefs are instead allowed to respond to desires. There is not the same difficulty in the case of those who benefit from the legitimating effect of their ideological desires on the economy. By contrast with the case of belief it needs little explanation that people's desires should slot in with their economic interests, that those who are advantaged by an economic system should have a reason to support it. For perceptions of interests are exactly the kind of thing to which we are normally disposed to respond practically. The only complication for a Marxist is in the idea of human interests. For if socialism serves more important human interests than the narrow economic interests which capitalism serves, then even those who benefit from a capitalist set-up would do better under socialism. Marx makes this point in the *Economic and Philosophic Manuscripts*, saying that socialism will bring 'a new enrichment of *human* nature'; by contrast, 'under private property ... Man becomes ever poorer as man'.[2] But this is not too much of a complication, for even if it is true that those who benefit from exploitation could be better off under another system, there is a clear sense in which they are nevertheless well off under this one—'where worker and capitalist equally suffer, the worker suffers in his very existence, the capitalist in the profit on his dead mammon'[3]—and that is quite enough to explain why they have the desires they have and support the economic system they do.

[2] *Economic and Philosphic Manuscripts*, p. 306.
[3] Ibid. 237.

The real problem concerns the people who benefit in no sense, not even the common-sense sense, from the entrenching effect of their values on the economic system. How do they acquire desires which are so massively out of touch with their interests and so suited to the interests of others? We need to consider some theories which might explain this. One suggested by Elster is that those who are the losers from an economic system resign themselves to their situation out of a frustration-reducing 'drive', their desires falling in with what is possible. This account exploits the facts about cognitive dissonance which I described in Ch. II. 4. The cognition, 'My lot in life is unpleasant', is dissonant with the cognition, 'I am stuck with it'. In order to reduce the dissonance, I convince myself that my situation is actually quite attractive. It is well known that people do this, minimizing the unpleasantness of their situation or exaggerating the desirability of what is inevitable, and Elster thinks it by far the most likely account of how the members of a subordinate class come to have the desires and goals which entrench the position of the ruling class.[4]

But we are looking for a history for their desires which is compatible with Marxism and the one proposed by Elster is not. Marxism says that it is the economy which determines ideology, that people have the desires and values which suit the economic regime because of the effect of the values on the regime, namely that they stabilize it. By contrast, Elster's version is that people have the desires and values which suit the regime because of the effect of those values on the people who have them, namely that adoption of them reduces their frustration. In other words, Elster's version eliminates the crucial contribution of the relations of production to the character of ideology, the fact that it is the relations of production which are explanatorily fundamental. It is true that on Elster's account there is an effect on the economy, for it would clearly suit the dominant class to have the dominated deal with their frustrations in this adaptive way. But since the operation of the dissonance-reducing mechanism is not

[4] Elster, *Sour Grapes*, p. 164.

explained by its benefits to the dominant class, its usefulness to them is sheer good fortune, merely a side-effect. Consequently dissonance reduction must be ruled out as a possible Marxist way for members of the subordinate class to acquire their ideological desires.

It might be wondered, since I deny here the applicability of dissonance theory to Marxism, how I could make use of it earlier when I claimed in Ch. II. 4 that it supports my argument that it is people's desire to think well of themselves which causes their false beliefs about their motives. The answer is that the dissonance there was between the bourgeoisie's image of themselves and their *economic* motives, so the effect on economic relations of reducing the dissonance was no accident. That is what the rationalization was *for*, to facilitate exploitation. But in the case I am discussing now, the dissonant desires have nothing to do with economic interests. The rationalization aims at comfort only, and its effect on economic relations is a windfall, pure luck.

Any account which depends on an emotional input from members of the subordinate class to explain their surrender to ideology is incompatible with Marxism for the same reason, that its effect on the economy will be coincidental. I am thinking of theories which postulate emotions in those who are oppressed, such as fear of the rulers, or a desire to conform, or to submit. Nietzsche's idea of resentment is an example. While the occurrence of such feelings might benefit the ruling class, that could only ever be an accident. Naturally, it would be different if the feelings were deliberately caused with a view to their advantages by members of the ruling class. Then they would be explained by their advantages. But that is implausible on other grounds, for it is hard to take seriously, as a candidate for a historical theory, the idea of a conspiracy that big. This is not to say that there is never deliberate propaganda behind the moulding of people's attitudes, for no doubt there often is an element of that—for instance, businesses putting out political advertisements—but only that that could never be the whole story. In any event, the conspiracy hypothesis does not fit with the Marxist doctrine that the members of the ruling class are not faking, that they accept, not merely pay lip-service to, the ideology. As Elster says, it is only occasionally that Marx denounces an opponent for conscious hypocrisy.[5]

We are looking for a theory which is both compatible with Marxism and not as off-beam as a conspiracy theory. The answer is to say that the unprofitable desires of members of the subordinate class are mostly the effect of a lifetime of social conditioning. On this theory, it is no coincidence that the desires of those who are exploited by the economic system should be so suited to it, for since it is the people with economic power who control the major institutions (church, school, press, and so on), it is naturally bourgeois attitudes, the attitudes which suit them, which those institutions will communicate. And there is no conspiracy, for the transmission of attitudes and values is normally quite automatic and happens without any deliberate intervention. The conservative values of the ruling class spread in a way which requires no effort from its members. Since they have power, they control access to opinion-forming institutions and their values inevitably get disseminated. The others are conditioned, but there is no conspiracy. The crucial text here is *The German Ideology*, in which Marx and Engels say:

The ideas of the ruling class are in every epoch the ruling ideas: i.e., the class which is the ruling *material* force of society is at the same time its ruling *intellectual* force. The class which has the means of material production at its disposal, consequently also controls the means of mental production, so that the ideas of those who lack the means of mental production are on the whole subject to it.[6]

And in the 'Manifesto of the Communist Party', Marx and Engels talk of the control which the bourgeoisie exercises over the major social institutions. They say of education, for instance: 'Is not that also social and determined by the social conditions under which you educate, by the intervention, direct or indirect, of society, by means of schools, etc?'[7] Gramsci is probably the Marxist theorist who has said most

[5] Elster, *Making Sense of Marx*, p. 465.
[6] *The German Ideology*, p. 59.
[7] 'Manifesto of the Communist Party', pp. 49–50.

about the moulding of working-class consciousness by institutions like religion, which disseminate the world-view of the
ruling class so effectively that it comes to take on the appearance of 'common sense'. The effect of this ideological and
cultural hegemony is to win the consent of the working class
to the dominance of the ruling class, effectively making a
revolution unthinkable, and therefore hitting on a much more
stable solution to the problem of maintaining domination
than the use of the state as an instrument of force and
repression.

Now that we have seen how ideological desires can arise, the
next thing to decide is whether they are defective because of
how they arise—that is, whether it is a defect in a desire that it
is conditioned.

I want to approach this question obliquely, beginning with
some observations about how the history of a belief is relevant
to its assessment, for certainly beliefs can be defective on
account of their history. There are, broadly speaking, three
points at which the history of a belief can be questioned. We
ask first whether the proposition believed could be arrived at
by the use of a reliable method; second, whether it was arrived
at by the use of a reliable method; and lastly, whether it was
the use of the method which verified it. The reason we cannot
stop at the first of these questions, but must go on to
investigate the second and third too, will be evident if one
reflects on the following facts: that I may hold a belief which
could be arrived at via a reliable method, although it was not
the use of such a method which caused me to hold it, and that
I can be justified in a belief although my belief is true by
accident only.

The reason these historical questions are important is
because there is a connection between history and truth. Of
course, a reliable method of acquisition is neither sufficient
nor necessary for truth, for a reliably acquired belief may be
false, and an unreliably acquired belief may be true. However,
a reliable method is guaranteed, at any rate, to lead to a high
proportion of true beliefs. Consulting tea leaves, for instance,
is less likely to yield true beliefs about the weather than
listening to the forecast on the radio, even though, in a particular case, the prediction arrived at through consulting the

leaves might happen to be the same as the one to be had from
the authority on the radio. Likewise, it detracts from the
likelihood of a belief's being true that there is not a causal connection between it and what makes it true.

What this shows is that the reason there is a right way to
acquire beliefs is because there is a way in which beliefs can go
wrong. For they go wrong when they are false and what is
suspect about some causes of belief is that they do away with
our general reason for thinking that a belief is true. An
example of a belief with a defective history, from Chapter II, is
a wishful belief. A belief caused by a desire can be at best
accidentally true.

Is conditioning a history which contaminates belief? Clearly.
For one thing, when we know someone has been conditioned
to accept a belief, we no longer have a general reason for
thinking it true. And there is also a second reason why a conditioned belief is suspect, which has to do with the fact that
there are systematic connections between beliefs. It would not
be possible for just one belief to be implanted in someone.
There would have to be adjustments made throughout the
system of beliefs. But the function of a belief is to represent
reality. Make enough adjustments, have enough of your beliefs
tinkered with, says Williams, and you may end up with total
destruction of reality.[8]

How is all this relevant to the question whether conditioning is the wrong kind of cause for a desire? Its relevance
is that, on analogy with belief, if there is a right way to acquire
desires we can expect that to be because there is a reliable way
to acquire the *right* desires. Now I argued in Ch. III. 7 that
desires go wrong when their object is not the agent's well-
being. So what requires to be investigated is whether there is a
way to acquire desires which is likely to yield beneficial
desires. If so, that will be the right way to acquire desires and
we shall be in a position to answer the question about conditioning.

A fruitful way to begin the investigation is to consider what
it is to have a character. Mill wrote perceptively about this,
saying that '[a person] whose desires and impulses are not his

[8] Williams, 'Deciding to Believe', p. 151.

own, has no character, no more than a steam-engine has a character'.[9] He explained that our desires and impulses are our own when they are the expression of our own nature. A person is like a tree, which needs to grow and develop 'according to the tendency of the inward forces which make it a living thing'.[10] Clearly this cannot mean, nor did Mill think it meant, that only a person uninfluenced by social and cultural forces has a character, for no one is uninfluenced by social and cultural forces. There would be nothing left to be the authentic self if its elements had to be radically unattached to the past to qualify as elements. That would be like expecting a tree to grow without water and sunlight. It is rather that certain *kinds* of influence make us reluctant to think of the ensuing wants and dispositions as an organic or authentic part of the self, in the way that a tree might be stunted by adding a certain chemical to the soil. The natural growth of the human personality requires intervention, but whereas some histories facilitate that growth, others obstruct the development in a person of desires and impulses which are in tune with inward inclinations. For instance, children brought up by normally reliable and sensitive parents have their dispositions and attitudes shaped in all sorts of ways, but the aim of the process is not to trim their characters to the needs of the parents; it is rather to make it possible for them eventually to establish themselves as persons and lead a life which uniquely suits their nature or real self. The opposite is the pathologically compliant person, who is caused by unfortunate early experiences to react uncritically and reflexively to environmental demands, and who is significantly described by psychoanalysts as having a 'false self'. Such people are incapable of 'the spontaneous gesture and the personal idea', and it is revealing that they feel unreal, or experience their own selves as unreal.[11] If there is nothing but the desire to do what others want or expect, there is a puppet in place of a real self.

If we compare the normal child-rearing process with, for instance, the frightening manipulation which wins new recruits to cults and creates bogus identifications, or if we

---

[9] Mill, *On Liberty*, p. 189.
[10] Ibid. 188.
[11] Winnicott, *The Maturational Processes and the Facilitating Environment*, p. 148.

consider advertising as a technique of influencing desires, big differences emerge. Marketers and merchandisers have always been disturbed by habits of thrift, and the fact that what we already have is often enough to satisfy us, and it is well known that they exploit the findings of psychologists and other social scientists to create 'fancied needs' in us. These 'merchants of discontent' are happy to admit that they use advertising 'to keep the masses dissatisfied with their mode of life, discontented with ugly things around them',[12] and to create irrational loyalties to products whose make-up does not differ from many other competing brands.[13] Success is measured in this world by the ability to effect changes in such things as the typical man's wardrobe, which 'once containing a blue serge, a black alpaca, a pair or two of shoes, one felt and straw hat, and a few odds and ends—today is bursting at the joints with Dacron, Orlon, nylon, blends, sports jackets, slacks, and colourful shorts, collections of hats for every occasion, and other varied paraphernalia'.[14] The trouble with desires caused in this way is that they seem to have nothing to do with us. They are alien grafts. And more frighteningly, when cult leaders manipulate potential new members by rigidly controlling their environment and what information gets through to them, and by playing on powerful feelings of guilt, shame, and fear, the effect is to destroy the victims' sense of separateness or identity, forcing them to betray their own impulses and retreat into total identification with the group. This kind of regression to all-or-nothing childish emotional identifications is called by Robert Lifton 'personal closure',[15] and it explains why the aim of those who attempt to 'deprogramme' cult members is precisely to restore their own conception of self.[16]

It might be thought that the case of political or social conditioning is different, because there do not seem to be any agents consciously aiming to manipulate the desires and attitudes of others. In fact it is a bit too simple to suppose that

---

[12] Ewen, *Captains of Consciousness*, p. 39.
[13] Packard, *The Hidden Persuaders*, p. 46.
[14] Ibid. 143.
[15] See Lifton, *Thought Reform and the Psychology of Totalism*, p. 421.
[16] Fleming, 'The Moral Status of Deprogramming', pp. 79–80.

there is never deliberate manipulation in the area of social control. Indeed, it is interesting that advertising has been deployed to exactly this end, business encouraging people to focus on the ever-enlarging possibilities of consumption as a way of deflecting attention from social issues, neutralizing class antagonisms, and pacifying. No wonder that advertising was declared in America to be 'the answer to Bolshevism'.[17] But I have already conceded that intentional manipulation is hard to take seriously, at any rate as the whole story about the shaping of the consciousness of the working class. Mostly it must be a question of the inevitable dissemination of attitudes and values which suit the capitalist class by the institutions they control. Is this a suspect history? Arguably, yes, for the influences to which people are subjected in capitalist society are both so narrow and so powerful as to make it unlikely that the outcome will be a character richly expressive of inward tendencies. Much more likely are the anaesthetized and one-dimensional individuals of whom Marcuse speaks. And, of course, feminists believe something analogous about women, that the intrusive conditioning of patriarchal society infantilizes women, habituates them to the accoutrements of cosmetics and fashion, to 'woman garbage', and turns them into 'fembots'.[18] There is so much more of which the human personality is capable—reflectiveness, creativity, open-mindedness, diversity—than the closed-minded obsessions with material goods, money, and fashion, and the conforming and custom-made forms of consciousness instilled by capitalism.

Finally, if we ask why it is that we are discomforted by the thought that our desires and attitudes might not be our own, might not be the outgrowth of our own individual characters, the only answer can be that such desires are unlikely to be directed to our interests and welfare. This is not to say that only desires directed to our own interests are our own desires: the connection is rather in the other direction, that desires which are not an expression of our real selves are unlikely to be synchronized with our interests. Mill explicitly made this connection, for he said that, 'Where not the person's own character, but the traditions or customs of other people are

[17] Ewen, *Captains of Consciousness*, p. 88.
[18] Grimshaw, 'Autonomy and Identity in Feminist Thinking', pp. 93, 102.

the rule of conduct, there is wanting one of the principal ingredients of human happiness'.[19] That must be right. Desires and motivations which are not an authentic expression of the self are unlikely to be integrated with a worthwhile life. It therefore follows that conditioning is the wrong kind of cause for desire because it is more likely, in stunting the development of character, to make desire go wrong. If the satisfaction of a conditioned desire makes the agent better off, that will be by coincidence only.

It is worth mentioning that there is a second way in which their ancestry is relevant to the assessment of ideological desires, and this is another point of analogy with belief. It is that with desires as with beliefs there is a system and coherence. Consequently you could never manufacture just one desire in someone: it would collide with others and make for incoherence. It is a global effect which has to be achieved. Indeed, since ideological values come in packages, a global effect is exactly what is achieved in the ideological case. But that should arouse our suspicions. Too much tinkering with belief will destroy reality; too much interference with a person's desires will destroy psychical integrity.

2. SOME MORE QUALMS ABOUT DESIRES

In the last section I said that the causation of ideological desires makes them suspect. In this section I want to discuss the Marxist view that they stand in the way of the agent's freedom, that although the victims of ideology may get what they want, their desires are an obstacle to their freedom. This is quite naturally described as the view that there can be 'internal' constraints on freedom,[20] but then a Marxist must be careful not to identify what is internal with what is a genuine part of the self, because, as we have just seen, desires which agents find in themselves are not necessarily *their* desires, not necessarily an authentic expression of their characters.

It would be satisfying if there were a connection between the causation and the freedom issues, the source of the desires

[19] Mill, *On Liberty*, p. 185.
[20] Lukes, *Marxism and Morality*, p. 72.

explaining why the agent is not free. But is it the case that desires which are not my own impede my freedom? In fact, I think a Marxist can argue this, although the connection has to be made quite carefully. For there is a way to make it which is compatible with Marxism and a way which is incompatible.

Someone might think, inspired by Heidegger, that our freedom consists in our control over our way of life and our capacity to choose what sort of person we will be. Conditioning, if it destroys the capacity to choose our way of life, will then erode freedom.

One problem with this is its excessively voluntarist account of character. It is tempting to argue against it that we no more choose our desires than we choose our beliefs, but that would be to exaggerate in the other direction, for it is true that we do sometimes make choices which at any rate influence what desires we come to have in the future. The trouble with such an account is rather that even when we do make such choices, the desire to make them is itself a function of an already existing character;[21] furthermore, there is room for freedom even without such choices, for when we act on desires we simply find in us, we are not necessarily unfree. In any event, a voluntarist account could not help a Marxist to make a connection between conditioning and lack of freedom. For on the voluntarist account as long as you have chosen your way of life, you are free. But on the Marxist account there are some ways of life which, whether chosen or not, are impediments to freedom. This is because a Marxist wants to tie freedom to the quality of a way of life: 'free activity', for the communists, is 'the creative manifestation of life arising from the free development of all abilities'.[22] It is the cultivation of gifts in all directions, a proliferation which is possible only in a certain kind of community.[23]

But then in what way can Marxism connect the source of a desire with its making for or blocking of freedom? The answer is that it can take its inspiration from Rousseau rather than Heidegger. Rousseau thought that when we desire to live in a

---

[21] See Galen Strawson's argument that self-determination as to desire is logically impossible (*Freedom and Belief*, pp. 28–9).

[22] *The German Ideology*, p. 225.

[23] Ibid. 78.

way which suits our nature, we are free, and loss of freedom is loss of the ability to lead a natural life. If that is true, Marxists would have a reason to say that conditioning erodes freedom, for, as I have already said, conditioned desires are not likely to be authentically connected with our natures. They are grafted on.

But is it plausible to think that freedom could have something to do with the conformity of a way of life to a person's nature? Those who believe that freedom is freedom to pursue whatever desires we happen to find in ourselves, will find it implausible, but I hope the following remarks will suggest the superficiality of their view.

We have the idea that some of our desires may be alien or foreign to us, and it seems that when we experience a desire as alien we also feel it is a restriction on our freedom. If we act on a desire which we experience as alien or with which we do not identify, and which we feel goes against what is good for us, all things considered, although we act intentionally, we may feel we would be freer were we free from the desire. Charles Taylor describes a few cases of this kind. If, for instance, I feel irrational fear of public speaking and am prevented from taking up a career I should find fulfilling, I may experience the fear as an obstacle; or spite may spoil a relationship which is tremendously important to me, and I may long to be free of the emotion; or I may experience my attachment to luxury and comfort as a restriction if it prevents me from doing certain things I would very much like to do, such as going on a demanding expedition.[24] It is in order to account for these kinds of case that Harry Frankfurt makes a distinction between acting freely, which is doing what you most want to do, or acting on your strongest desire, and having free will, which is what you have when the will you have is the will you want to have. You have free will, according to Frankfurt, when the desires by which you are moved are the desires by which you desire to be moved.[25]

Frankfurt's is an inviting view because it allows for freedom of the will while not denying that our desires and values and attitudes might be the outcome of influences over which we

[24] Taylor, 'What's Wrong with Negative Liberty?', p. 185.
[25] Frankfurt, 'Freedom of the Will and the Concept of a Person', p. 15.

have had no control. It accomplishes this by tying freedom of the will to the ratification or endorsement of motivations we find in ourselves, rather than to anything about their origin or nature. On this view, it does not matter how you acquired your motivations; as long as you reflect on them and endorse them you will enjoy freedom of the will. But this account could never be acceptable to a Marxist, for the victims of an ideology may identify with the ideological desires by which they are moved, and do not necessarily feel that those desires go against what is good for them, all things considered. On Frankfurt's analysis we would be obliged to take their feelings at face value, whereas a Marxist would want to question them, on the basis that your attitude to the desires which move you can itself be infected or corrupted by ideology. Marcuse implicitly makes this point, for he says that 'The people recognize themselves in their commodities; they find their soul in their automobile, hi-fi set, split-level home, kitchen equipment'.[26] The result is 'euphoria in unhappiness',[27] 'repressive satisfaction'.[28] Consequently a Marxist needs to show that Frankfurt is wrong and that whether you have free will is not fundamentally a matter of your attitude to your will, not a matter of endorsing the desires by which you are moved. It must be shown that it is not necessary to experience your desires as foreign and obstructive to suffer a reduction in your freedom; it would rather be the fact that they are objectively foreign which reduces your freedom. Can that be shown?

In fact, I think it can be. Those who work with ill people are quick to see that freedom is connected with enjoying an effectively functioning personality. The neurologist, Oliver Sacks, for instance, describes how neurological disorders can have an impact on people's freedom. There is a disease called 'Tourette's syndrome', in which a disturbance in the primitive parts of the brain causes an 'excitement of the emotions and the passions',[29] and which is associated with a particular kind of personality, one given to extravagant and excited movements, to obscenities, to abnormally accelerated and indiscriminate

---

[26] Marcuse, *One-Dimensional Man*, p. 9.
[27] Ibid. 5.
[28] Ibid. 7.
[29] Sacks, *The Man who Mistook his Wife for a Hat*, p. 90.

associations and reactions, and to weird and inventive kinds of humour. What is it to suffer from such a disease? One of Sacks's Tourette's patients explains that it is to suffer from a reduction in freedom:

> You 'normals', who have the right transmitters in the right places at the right times in your brains, have all feelings, all styles, available all the time—gravity, levity, whatever is appropriate. We Touretters don't: we are forced into levity by our Tourette's and forced into gravity when we take haldol. You are free, you have a natural balance: we must make the best of an artificial balance.[30]

But it is not only organic disorders which can undermine freedom. To be in an ill state of mind can obviously have the same effect, and successful psychotherapy can restore freedom, by enlarging choices and enabling a person to be less ruled by inhibitions, compulsions, and irrational emotions like guilt or anxiety or fear.

Now, since it is an objective matter whether you suffer from a less than effectively functioning personality, it cannot be essential that your condition should be experienced as a restriction on your freedom for it to be a restriction. The point is that we can be mistaken about what is foreign to us and therefore a fetter on our wills, and we are made less free by anxieties and neuroses and the disruptive effects on personality of disease whether we are aware of their restricting effects on our lives or not. The relevant test would seem to be not whether you distance yourself from or repudiate the causes of your actions, but rather whether loss of those elements of your personality would be a gain for you, even if, were the desires and motivations to be retained, they would be satisfied. Taylor argues on somewhat the same lines, for he says that people's aspirations may be, unknown to them, confused by the sort of emotion mentioned earlier—spite and irrational fear—so that they lose nothing in losing these emotions, while everything truly important to them is safeguarded.[31]

Obviously there can be, and are, different criteria of psychological health. For psychoanalysts, for instance, it is emotional maturity, adaptability, and independence. It will come as no

---

[30] Sacks, *The Man who Mistook his Wife for a Hat*, p. 96.
[31] Taylor, 'What's Wrong with Negative Liberty?', p. 192.

surprise that for Marx it is connected with his picture of
human nature, on which the ability to lead a rich, creative, and
versatile life is conceived as the psychologically natural state
for us, and effective functioning therefore requires the 'all-
round development of all [one's] abilities'.[32] It follows that dispositions and motives at odds with the multi-dimensional
cultivation of all our talents—the one-sided and compulsive
desires imposed by capitalism, the driving passion for money,
the morbid avarice—are foreign to us and burden our wills.
There may be objections to this picture of psychological well-
being, but it is not a picture I have particularly tried to defend.
My arguments support the more general view that desires
which sabotage the effective functioning of our personalities,
whatever those may actually be, restrict our freedom.

*

Drawing the arguments of this chapter together, Marxism can
marshal a lot of support for its qualms about ideological
desires. An economical way of putting it is to say that ideological desires are rogue, for that phrase suggests both the
defects disclosed. First, their causation is abnormal, and
second, they are destructive of our freedom. The connection is
that desires which are abnormally caused are likely to be
foreign to our nature, impediments to whatever is effective
psychological functioning for us, and that means they are
likely to diminish our freedom.

One final point is that all I have said in this chapter about
false consciousness and freedom is compatible with the truth
of determinism. For it is an implication of my argument that
certain ways of influencing people's characters and dispositions are likely to produce individuals who enjoy freedom.

[32] *The German Ideology*, p. 292.

V

Recidivist Beliefs and Desires

1. COGNITIVE ILLUSIONS

I have discussed two ideological errors, the mistake of the bourgeoisie about their motives and the mistake of the workers about what is good for them. But of course there are also many false beliefs about less obscure matters which are also branded ideological by Marx. The taint of ideology attaches, for instance, to the belief that workers dispose voluntarily of their labour power, that they are not forced to work; to the belief that capital can be the source of profit; and to the belief that market forces are natural forces and operate independently of human intentions. A more recherché example of an ideological belief is the belief that commodities possess exchange value naturally, that they have it just by virtue of being the things they are, rather than by virtue of being social objects, depositories of human labour power. These and others play on various themes: taking what is social for what is natural; imagining that things which do not have power do; thinking that what can be avoided is inevitable and what really is compelled is free. One interesting claim which Marx makes about such beliefs—and it is this claim which will be the subject of discussion in this chapter—is that evidence that they are false does nothing to exorcise the 'illusions', just so long as society continues to be organized in the same way. He says, for instance, that 'the demand to give up illusions about the existing state of affairs is the demand to give up a state of affairs which needs illusions',[1] and that:

The recent scientific discovery that labour products, as values, are but the material expressions of the human labour expended in their production, marks an epoch in the evolutionary history of mankind, but does not suffice to dispel the semblance of materiality which has

---

[1] Introduction to *Contribution to the Critique of Hegel's Philosophy of Law*, p. 176.

been assumed by the social character of labour. Physical and chemical science have analysed air into its elements, but the familiar bodily impressions produced on our senses by the atmosphere persist unchanged.[2]

The analogy is bad, for there is no reason why 'bodily impressions' *should* alter, given knowledge of the chemical composition of air. That would be like expecting someone who has learnt that physical objects are not solid to refuse to put a pencil on the table. But the underlying idea is unaffected, namely, that theory does not 'dispel the semblance'.

But how should we interpret that idea? There are a couple of ways to interpret it which raise few philosophical problems and one way which raises many.

It would be relatively unproblematic if the ideological beliefs were merely 'half-believed' in H. H. Price's sense. That is: if they were believed on some occasions but not on others. Price's example is of a man who has a genuinely religious attitude but only on Sundays.[3] Likewise we might suppose that the victims of ideology lead a kind of double intellectual life. When they reason 'scientifically', to use Marx's phrase, they see where the evidence points and reject the ideological beliefs. At other times, though, when they are under the sway of the ideology, they forget about the evidence. It flies out of the window. And at that moment the beliefs take hold.

A second unproblematic interpretation of Marx's claim that theory does not dispel the semblance would be that the ideological beliefs continue merely to *seem* true to those who now, after reading Marx, think them false. 'Science' penetrates the appearances in the same way that a ruler puts you right about the length of the Muller–Lyer lines. Though you believe the ideology is false, it will still appear true to you, in just the way that though you know the lines are unequal they still seem equal. Cohen interprets Marx in this way, for he says, 'Things do not *seem* different to a worker who knows Marxism. He knows they *are* different from the way they continue to seem to be.'[4]

---

[2] *Capital*, i. 47–8. I have chosen the Everyman translation as being clearer.
[3] Price, *Belief*, pp. 305–6.
[4] Cohen, *Karl Marx's Theory of History*, p. 331.

On a third and controversial reading, by contrast, it is actual belief which survives scientific thought. This interpretation shares with the first interpretation the idea that by 'illusion' Marx meant actual belief and with the second the idea that the illusion operates alongside the evidence and not intermittently. It is a matter of subjects' being unaffected by evidence whose significance they recognize.

It will help to clarify the implications of these interpretations if we examine Marx's explanation of the persistence of ideological illusions. It has to do with his belief that economic conditions generate misleading appearances, and it will be useful to give some of his examples. Marx tells us, for instance, that although 'the wage-labourer is bound to his owner by invisible threads',[5] the fact that workers are always, in capitalist society, bargaining and contracting over the sale of their labour power creates the illusion that they are free. 'The appearance of independence is kept up by means of a constant change of employers, and by the fictio juris of a contract.'[6] Again, the reason that commodities have exchange value is because of the labour expended on them. Yet they appear to have value intrinsically, independent of the labour process. This is an example of what Marx calls 'fetishism' in the famous section of *Capital* headed 'The Fetishism of Commodities and the Secret Thereof'. Marx claims that 'this ultimate money-form of the world of commodities . . . actually conceals, instead of disclosing, the social character of private labour, and the social relations between the individual producers'.[7] Also: 'the relation of the producers to the sum total of their own labour is presented to them as a social relation, existing not between themselves, but between the products of their labour.'[8] So the expression of a product's value in terms of its money value, rather than in terms of how much labour was expended on it, makes it appear as if its value is an intrinsic property. And because, in commodity production, individual producers are brought into relation with each other only via the products of their labour, it appears as if the social

[5] *Capital*, i. 538.
[6] Ibid.
[7] Ibid. 80.
[8] Ibid. 77.

relations are between objects, rather than people. A third example of how appearances mislead is the way in which, under capitalism, 'All labour appears as paid labour'[9] and so exploitation is concealed. The workers are exploited in so far as there is a difference between the cost of their labour power and the value which it creates. But the capitalist appears to pay not for the labour power, but for the labour. 'We see', Marx writes, that

The value . . . by which a part only of the working-day . . . is paid for, appears as the value or price of the whole working-day . . . , which thus includes . . . hours unpaid for. The wage-form thus extinguishes every trace of the division of the working-day into necessary labour and surplus-labour, into paid and unpaid labour . . . the money relation conceals the unrequited labour of the wage-labourer.[10]

Now someone might think that there is a connection between these examples and the second interpretation, which is that the ideological beliefs continue merely to seem true to those who, having read Marx, now think them false. The reason would be this: if it looks as if workers are free, and commodities have value intrinsically, and all labour is paid labour, that must be in the sense in which a straight stick looks bent in water. But it would be mad to carry on believing the stick is bent after discovering that it is straight. Likewise it cannot be possible to read Marx, accept that the weight of the evidence is against your beliefs, and persist in them. At most they will continue merely to seem true in the way that the stick continues to seem bent.

Clearly, this argument for the second interpretation hangs on the promising-looking analogy between ideological and perceptual illusions, and an argument for the third interpretation—that ideological beliefs may continue actually to be thought true by those who acknowledge evidence that suggests they are false—would need to dispute that. But there is no need for a proponent of the third interpretation to deny that there are *any* points of similarity. Evidently there are, and they arise from the fact that the errors are generated by

---

[9] Ibid. 505.
[10] Ibid.

economic practices. The points of analogy between ideological errors and perceptual illusions which the third interpretation can accommodate are these: first, both are what I
describe in the next section as 'passive'. This has to do with
their persistence or tenacity. Second, in neither case is it some
idiosyncrasy or abnormality of the agent which accounts for
their persistence. It needs not a change in the agent but a
change in the world to extirpate ideological misconceptions.
As Marx says about commodity fetishism, it is 'inseparable
from the production of commodities'.[11]

A proponent of the third interpretation might even call
ideological errors 'cognitive illusions' on account of the
similarities they share with perceptual illusions—provided that
'illusion' is understood broadly, and not as something weaker
than belief, and provided also that there is no confusion with
the illusions called 'cognitive' by cognitive psychologists. The
Gambler's Fallacy, for instance, which is often called a cognitive illusion by psychologists, is not tenacious. It is normal
for people untutored in statistics to be guilty of it but once
exposed it has no tendency to persist. Ideological errors, by
contrast, tend not to be dislodged.

I have said that a proponent of the third interpretation,
which says that it is actual belief which survives Marx's disclosures, can allow that there are some points of similarity
between the resistant beliefs and perceptual illusions. What
must be denied, however, is that ideological illusions are
tenacious in the very same sense that perceptual illusions are
tenacious. For the tenacity in the perceptual case extends only
as far as an *experience*. I shall say more about this later, but the
main point is that although your evidence that the thing is an
illusion cannot prevent you from experiencing it as real, it
must destroy your belief that it is real. The impact of the
evidence is completely and immediately to cancel belief. By
contrast, in the ideological case the tenacity is the tenacity of
belief against the weight of recognized contrary evidence. At
any rate, that is the third interpretation.

As to which interpretation Marx actually had in mind, it is
hard to say. I think it possible that he meant to make the third,

[11] *Capital*, i. 77.

more ambitious claim. The first interpretation is not really a serious candidate: nowhere does Marx suggest that ideological beliefs come and go, so it is completely unsupported by textual evidence. One could find ample evidence to support the second, but there is also support for the third—in the Everyman edition of *Capital*, for instance, Eden and Cedar Paul translate the rest of the paragraph from which I have already quoted as follows:

after the discovery of the true nature of value, no less than before, those entangled in the meshwork of commodity production regard as universally valid a truth which is in fact true only for one particular form of production, namely commodity production. They continue to believe without qualification that the specifically social character of mutually independent acts of individual or private labour consists in their general likeness as human labour, and assumes in the labour product the characteristic form of value.[12]

But whether Marx meant to be understood in that way or not, I want to defend its coherence. Later I shall argue that it is consistent with Marxism, for I think it is a mistake to think that if it is true that ideological beliefs reflect the way things seem, that must be because there is an exact analogy between ideological beliefs and perceptual illusions. I shall resuscitate Marx's various examples of the world's appearing a certain way and show how they can just as well be put to work in the service of the third interpretation. But quite apart from that, I want to defend the third interpretation because I think it is in general possible that evidence should be resisted by belief. If it seems impossible, that is because we tend to overlook the many ways in which the intellect can fail us. Cardinal Newman was someone who was not guilty of that, for he saw that beliefs may be too strong for the intellect, saying that sometimes 'good arguments, and really good as far as they go, and confessed by us to be good, nevertheless are not strong enough to incline our minds ever so little to the conclusion at which they point'.[13] I want to argue that Newman was right.

Of course, as I have already said, in Ch. II. 5, it is possible for a *wish* consciously to cause belief against the weight of

---

[12] Ibid. 48 (Everyman edn.).
[13] Quoted in Price, *Belief*, p. 135.

acknowledged evidence. But there cannot be a desire contributing to the ideological beliefs I am interested in now. The false beliefs I was talking about there suited the subjects: the topic was beliefs which cater to self-image. But here the false beliefs are held even by those whom it does not suit. Beliefs about freedom, the market, exploitation, and so on, grip capitalists and workers alike. But the latter derive no benefit from them. Consequently a Marxism which opts for the third interpretation will need to ascribe the resilience of the beliefs to the contribution of factors other than desire.[14] In fact I think that there *are* factors besides desire or the impulse to deny some painful fact which can dispose us to belief in defiance of conclusions that reasoning insists on. Psychology is full of examples of people failing to be affected by evidence relevant to their beliefs, and in the next section I shall describe some of them and say what bearing they have on the philosophical problems raised by the third interpretation of Marx's claims.

Satisfyingly analogous to the claim that ideological beliefs are able to survive recognized contrary evidence is one of the conclusions of Chapter III about ideological desires, namely that they are able to survive a negative valuation, and later I shall say more about the points of analogy. I shall be looking at some belief-inducing and will-disposing factors, not only for the support they lend an interpretation of Marx, but also for the pay-off in the other direction, for the light that is cast on some intriguing but neglected mental states.

2. SOME EXAMPLES

Here are some experimental findings of psychologists.

Introductory psychology students intending to major in psychology were provided with one of two forms of information about psychology courses. Some were given statistical

---

[14] Mele argues that there is a phenomenon which he calls 'doxastic incontinence', which involves non-irresistible belief in *p*, despite a conscious judgement to the effect that there is good and sufficient reason for not believing *p*. However, he argues that the phenomenon occurs because of the subject's 'conative condition'. In particular, the belief is motivated (see ch. 8 of *Irrationality*). Contrast the phenomenon in which I am interested.

information—actual mean evaluations based on the reports of all the students who had taken the course in the previous term. Others had face-to-face reports about the courses from a small and unrepresentative number of students. Both groups were then asked to say what courses they intended to take and how confident they were about their choices. It was found that the face-to-face information had a greater effect on the students' plans and their confidence in their choices.[15]

Two purportedly authentic studies differing in their conclusion on the deterrent value of capital punishment were presented to university students, some of whom believed strongly that capital punishment had a deterrent effect, the rest believing strongly that it did not. One of the studies compared murder rates for states before and after the adoption of capital punishment. The other compared murder rates during the same period of time for states with and states without capital punishment. The students found whichever study supported their own position to be more convincing and better designed than the opposing study. In other words, their willingness to question the evidence depended quite straightforwardly on whether it supported or threatened their position.[16]

Subjects told that, 'While dancing, Ralph trips over Joan's feet', and asked whether the tripping was Ralph's fault, Joan's fault, or due to the circumstances, were influenced by information about whether Ralph trips over most girls' feet and whether he usually trips over Joan's feet but apparently found it irrelevant that other people might trip over Joan's feet.[17]

Subjects who read an essay in favour of—or against—the legalization of marijuana or Castro's leadership of Cuba concluded that the essay expressed the writer's beliefs even though it had been made clear to them that the writer had had no choice about what was written. And when subjects were told that an essay they had listened to had not been written by the speaker, they nevertheless concluded that the views expressed in the essay were the speaker's views.[18]

---

[15] Nisbett and Ross, *Human Inference*, p. 58.
[16] Ibid. 170.
[17] Nisbett *et al.*, 'Popular induction', pp. 102–3.
[18] Freedman *et al.*, *Social Psychology*, pp. 153–5.

Finally, high-school pupils were asked to solve mathematical puzzles. Half of them had received a clear, coherent lecture that provided the technique to solve the puzzles; the others merely a 'rambling and unhelpful series of exhortations'. Unsurprisingly, the first group performed very well, the second group poorly. Half the pupils in each group were then meticulously 'debriefed' on the cause of their performance, the experimenter analysing the superiority or inferiority of the lecture they had received. All the pupils then judged their abilities for the task, their liking for it, and their probable future performance. Both the pupils who had been debriefed, and those who had not, rated their ability according to their initial experience of success or failure.[19]

What is the significance of these examples? Psychologists tend to say that they show that 'information is not necessarily informative',[20] or that people are 'unresponsive' to information,[21] or that they 'resist' it,[22] but these terms are multiply ambiguous and in fact it appears that the experiments establish different things. There are at least three ways in which you can fail to be affected by evidence relevant to your beliefs: you might irrationally fail to register or see the relevance of the evidence; you might irrationally reject the evidence; or you might acknowledge the evidence but irrationally persist in your beliefs. If we now look at the experiments again we can see that all of these things happened.

How, for instance, should we explain the fact that subjects asked to infer why Ralph tripped over Joan's feet were mostly affected by information about Ralph's behaviour and hardly affected by information about others' behaviour? The psychologists say that information about people other than the actor is more indirect than information about the actor and its relevance to the required inference is therefore harder to grasp.

Learning anything about the actor from such information requires an inference of a rather roundabout sort—from knowledge of (a) the

[19] Nisbett and Ross, *Human Inference*, p. 179.
[20] Nisbett *et al.*, 'Popular induction', p. 101.
[21] Nisbett and Ross, *Human Inference*, p. 132.
[22] Freedman *et al.*, *Social Psychology*, p. 155.

behaviour of other people to inferences about (b) the X-evoking properties of the stimulus to inferences about (c) the effects of the X-evoking properties of the stimulus on the particular actor.[23]

If this is the right explanation, what is described is clearly a case of failing to register rather than rejecting or, *a fortiori*, recognizing relevant evidence and persisting in your belief. The wrong step is taken at a very early point.

It looks as if the same thing might be true of the subjects who inappropriately weighted the statistical and the face-to-face evidence about psychology courses, that is, that they too failed to register relevant evidence, perhaps because people tend to be disinclined to attend to statistical information. In fact, however, the experimenters made use of various checks which showed that the subjects were not only exposed to the statistics but also *absorbed* them,[24] which means that the case actually belongs in the third category mentioned above, the category of beliefs which defy recognized evidence. The explanation of the defiance, according to the psychologists, is the greater vividness and concreteness of face-to-face over superior but pallid statistical evidence. Its vividness is supposed to account for its inappropriate impact on inferences.[25]

What about the other examples? The students with the strong views about capital punishment, who only saw the design flaws in the study which threatened their views, were clearly challenging or discrediting evidence rather than recognizing or acknowledging it. This case belongs with phenomena like blanket rejection of evidence and what psychologists call 'derogation of the source of information', by which they mean attacking an opponent as unreliable or delinquent, or otherwise discreditable.[26]

That leaves the subjects with the irrational beliefs about a speaker's or writer's views and the pupils who could not be successfully debriefed about the cause of their poor performance at a puzzle-solving task. These, like the statistics case, are cases of belief resisting acknowledged evidence. The pupils who had been debriefed absorbed the evidence, for they were

---

[23] Nisbett and Ross, *Human Inference*, pp. 133–4.
[24] Ibid. 59.
[25] Ibid. 55–9.
[26] Freedman *et al.*, *Social Psychology*, pp. 364–5.

able to predict accurately how others exposed to the two lectures would perform at the task.[27] And the same must be true of the subjects who read and listened to the essays, for they did not challenge the evidence nor was there anything standing in the way of its being registered. Its import was completely plain and on the surface. So the information was registered but not appropriately utilized in inference.

This much is psychology. But what is the relevance of these findings to the philosophical problem? Psychology tells us that beliefs sometimes fail to be affected by relevant evidence, and I said that there are actually three ways in which that could happen: the evidence might not be registered; it might be rejected; or it might be recognized but not have the appropriate impact on inference. On the interpretation of Marx whose coherence I want to defend, the failure of ideological beliefs to be affected by relevant evidence must happen in the last of the ways just described. This is because Marx talks about theoretical *discoveries* not affecting ideological ways of thought and says that subjects can remain in the grip of illusions which their criticism has *dissolved*: 'even the best spokesmen of classical economy remain more or less in the grip of the world of illusion which their criticism had dissolved.'[28] You cannot reject or fail to register what you have seen through and discovered. Incidentally, this text and others which use similar phrases provide an extra kind of evidence that Marx wanted to be understood in the way the third interpretation suggests he did. For he is talking about the economists in their capacity as spokesmen and there would be no reason for them, as spokesmen, to describe how the world merely seems to them. Spokesmen present their beliefs. In any event, the main point here is that the only way to make the interpretation on which 'illusion' means 'belief' consistent with Marx's usage of phrases like 'scientific discovery' is to suppose that he is saying that someone might judge that all the evidence favours a certain conclusion yet believe the opposite— that is, that the relevant evidence is recognized but fails to have the appropriate impact on inference, the third way of failing to affect belief which I mentioned.

---

[27] Nisbett and Ross, *Human Inference*, p. 179.
[28] *Capital*, iii. 830.

It will help to introduce some terminology here. Sometimes mental phenomena fail to be governed by other mental phenomena and when the failure is conscious it is appropriate to say that the one kind of mental phenomenon is passive in respect of the other. Sensations, for instance, are passive in respect of beliefs, unaffected by beliefs, except in those very marginal cases in which people manage to alter their experience of pain by their attitude to it. An example of a sensation unalterable by belief is the sensation experienced by amputees in their phantom limbs. Perceptions are also insensitive to beliefs. How things look is constrained by the cues and except in cases of ambiguity our response is triggered automatically. This is why perceptual illusions persist, in the face of the belief that the experience misrepresents its object. Suppose you are looking at a *trompe-l'œil* ceiling painting from the point at which it manages to contrive the impression that the architecture of the building continues. Or suppose, to make use of an example of Gombrich's, that you are looking through a box which opens on a Fantin-Latour still life, and the lighting is so arranged that the table, flowers, and fruit look real.[29] Then even when you know that it is a flat ceiling or a picture at which you are looking, that will not touch your experience, your perception of something three-dimensional. We can even perceive impossible objects, as the drawings of Escher, which present incompatible spatial information, show.

There is a fact about belief which can also be put in terms of passivity. The fact is, as Williams says, that we cannot consciously decide to believe.[30] This can be put in terms of the notion of passivity by saying that belief is passive in respect of, or independent of, the workings of the will. Contrast imagination which is, as Wittgenstein points out, a will-governed activity. 'There is such an order as "Imagine this".'[31]

Now what the third interpretation of Marx claims is that there is an additional respect in which belief can be passive, for it can be passive in relation to reasoning.

It is tempting to bring in the findings of the psychologists directly now and say that they show that that interpretation is

---

[29] Gombrich, *Art and Illusion*, p. 233.
[30] Williams, 'Deciding to Believe', pp. 147–51.
[31] Wittgenstein, *Philosophical Investigations* II, p. 213.

defensible, but that would be to misinterpret their relevance. They record cases in which belief *is* passive in respect of reasoning—and that is part of their importance because many philosophers are too quick to deny that such irrationality can happen. But they have no bearing on the question, which any defender of the third interpretation of Marx's claim must answer, how passivity in that respect is possible. The right answer to that question is rather the philosophical one that, because of the nature of inductive reasoning, it is not impossible for belief to be passive in respect of it. Just because the evidence is not deductive there is a gap between it and the conclusion it warrants and that gap gives a person enough space to form the unwarranted conclusion. I mentioned in Ch. II. 5 that Pears calls this space 'latitude', and points out that it is in the nature of inductive evidence that it gives people the latitude they need in order to evade it.[32]

The findings of the psychologists remind us not to be too quick to say what can and cannot happen. They document systematically kinds of cases which, when we reflect further, we realize are familiar in everyday life. They are also important in a second way in that it would be interesting to know why ideological beliefs should defy the verdict of the intellect. Psychology ought to be an aid here for it aims to discover the factors which dispose us irrationally to belief.

Probably the most obvious belief-disposing factor is desire. But we know that there cannot be a desire contributing to the ideological beliefs which are the subject of this discussion. I have already supplied the reasons. For one thing, it needs a change in the world, not a change in people's affective constitutions, to dissolve the ideological beliefs. Second, there is nothing to be gained by those who are exploited from the resilience of their beliefs. They have no motive to believe the ideology. So in their case, at any rate, there must be some causal influence at work other than desire.

What, then, might the relevant belief-disposing factor be? This is really where the psychological findings come into their own because in none of the cases I described, in which evi-

---

[32] Pears, *Motivated Irrationality*, pp. 75–6.

dence whose significance was recognized failed properly to be utilized, did motivational factors play any role. They probably played a role in the capital punishment experiment but that was not a case in which the significance of the evidence was recognized. Mostly the tenacious belief in the relevant cases was neutral but in at least one of the cases the belief was actually unflattering—the case of the pupils who performed poorly at the puzzle-solving task and continued to think of themselves as incompetent even when the cause of their lack of success had been elaborately indicated. I have already mentioned one of the factors which the psychologists say may bias belief: people's inferences are more influenced by vivid or salient than by weightier but pallid information. It will be remembered that it was its lack of concreteness and interest that accounted for the failure of statistical information to affect the students' inferences about psychology courses. Likewise, in the essay experiment, the psychologists say that the subjects could not believe that external pressures on the writer or speaker had influenced the views expressed, because their experience of the writer's or speaker's behaviour (of the writing or speaking) was so salient that it 'engulfed the field' for them.[33]

In the case of unsuccessful attempts to debrief people who have been subjects in psychology experiments, factors like the following may play a part: earlier presented information has an effect out of proportion to its weight;[34] people tend to understand the concept of confirmation more easily than that of disconfirmation and search out confirming evidence;[35] we are quick to generate explanations for events such as poor performance at a task, and once generated the explanations acquire a life of their own and are very hard to shift.[36]

These are some of the non-motivational factors which can push belief in the wrong direction. The hope is that they will help to throw light on the ideological case.

[33] Freedman *et al.*, *Social Psychology*, p. 153.
[34] Nisbett and Ross, *Human Inference*, p. 172.
[35] Ibid. 181.
[36] Ibid. 183–6.

3. IDEOLOGICAL BELIEFS

In the ideological case there is theory saying one thing and all a person's experience saying another. Marx tells us that capitalism restricts freedom and that wage contracts are coercive, but all our institutions presuppose a connection between freedom and dealing with property or selling labour. Likewise, Marx may tell people that they share class interests while all their experience is of separation and isolation. There is a famous passage in *The Eighteenth Brumaire* in which Marx discusses why the French peasantry should have favoured Louis Napoleon Bonaparte and explains that the peasants failed to act as a class because their experience gave them no reason to believe that they were members of one. Although it is obvious to us that they shared interests, their poverty, their lack of means of communication, and their solitary cultivation of isolated smallholdings made it very difficult for them to see that.

A smallholding, a peasant and his family; alongside them another smallholding, another peasant and another family. A few score of these make up a village, and a few score of villages make up a department. In this way the great mass of the French nation is formed by simple addition of homologous magnitudes, much as potatoes in a sack form a sack of potatoes.[37]

Again, Marx tells us that the belief that the worker's wage is the price of labour arises from influential everyday experiences. The exchange between capital and labour resembles the exchange of any other commodity, and so it is natural to think that labour has a price.[38] What is more, the category 'price of labour' is enshrined in everyday language,[39] an imprimatur which will have an obvious tendency to increase the biasing effect of experience. A fourth example, this time from the work of Lukács, is the experience of the legal system and the state as legitimate: 'the organs of authority harmonize to such an extent with the (economic) laws governing men's lives, or seem so overwhelmingly superior that men experience them as natural forces, as the necessary environment for

[37] *The Eighteenth Brumaire of Louis Bonaparte*, p. 187.
[38] *Capital*, i. 506.
[39] Ibid. 503.

their existence.'[40] The examples of this kind of thing could be multiplied, their common element being the fact of skewed experience.

The same thing happens, I think, with racist and sexist stereotypes. The stereotypes are deeply rooted in institutions, unhesitatingly assumed day after day in books, television, and advertisements. They are just like the solidly established attitudes and beliefs with which the theory of ideology deals: early ingrained attitudes to property and property trans-actions, to different kinds of economic system, and so on.

Incidentally, I think that this idea, of experiences being biased or skewed, supplies a way to make sense of some quite enigmatic comments made by Marx. Sometimes Marx tells us that the reason people have false beliefs is because the *world* is distorted and reality topsy-turvy. For instance, although we know from the theory of fetishism that social relations 'assume the fantastic form' of a relation between things, Marx also says, enigmatically, that the social relations 'really are' 'material relations between persons and social relations between things'.[41] Likewise we are told that though capital appears to possess objectified labour, yet 'this twisting and inversion is a *real* [phenomenon], not a merely *supposed one* existing merely in the imagination of the workers and the capitalists'.[42] If we take this literally, we land in contradiction: the ideological beliefs which were all along false now also turn out to be true. Perhaps this is why some Marxists deny that ideology has anything to do with false belief. Ideology provides, they say, not a distorted picture of the world, but a true picture of a distorted world. But for those who are baffled by distorted worlds, there is another way to resolve the paradox: our experience of reality is biased and the false beliefs accurately describe the experience, not reality.

But that is not enough to explain why the false beliefs should be so stubborn in the face of Marx's disclosures. I think the defender of Marx can draw on the findings of the psycho-logists now and say that the experience is so vivid that it is able to take over and emasculate Marx's theoretical disclosures.

---

[40] Lukács, *History and Class Consciousness*, p. 257.
[41] *Capital*, i. 78.
[42] *Grundrisse*, p. 831.

The theory has difficulty engaging with the beliefs—it has as much influence on them as, to use Freud's famous phrase, 'a distribution of menu-cards in a time of famine has upon hunger'.[43]

Another factor which probably plays a role here and contributes to theory's defeat is that the application of the theoretical evidence is so complicated. 'A fatiguing climb',[44] according to Marx, is necessary for anyone intending to gain the summits of science—so fatiguing, indeed, that Isaac Deutscher was led to wonder whether Marx had not made the pathways too steep.[45] The point I want to make here is that theoretical evidence is more likely to have its expected influence on beliefs when its application is simple; as the issues become more complicated and abstract there is more room for the overwhelming impact of contrary and vivid experience to push belief in the wrong direction.

I have already said that racial and sexual stereotypes are like ideological beliefs in being deeply rooted in social institutions. Like ideological beliefs they are also notoriously hard to dislodge. It is therefore a natural speculation that the explanation of their fantastic insensitivity to information could be the same: theoretical evidence that the stereotypes have no foundation in reality has difficulty engaging with them in the presence of pervasive, and more psychologically accessible, experiential evidence suggesting otherwise.

I have made a lot of the difference between theoretical and experiential evidence but I must now mention a possible confusion. I can best explain it by supposing that someone would like to gloss what I have said as follows: 'It is true that recognized theoretical evidence does not necessarily engage with beliefs. It happens all the time—for instance, with people who say they believe aeroplanes are safe, yet refuse to fly. Such people appreciate the evidence theoretically or intellectually, merely, rather than in the gut or at heart.' My interlocutor identifies theoretical evidence which does not have the expected impact with evidence which is appreciated merely intellectually. The thought is that evidence needs to make a

---

[43] Freud, '"Wild" Psychoanalysis', Standard Edition, xi. 225.
[44] Preface to the French edn. of *Capital*, i, at p. 30.
[45] Deutscher, *Marxism in Our Time*, p. 257.

visceral connection if it is to have the expected impact. But I am suspicious of this idea. When you try to pin the metaphor down, its meaning proves fugitive. It is not as if, in one kind of case, evidence has an inferior, cerebral effect, whereas in the standard case evidence has a visceral effect. In the standard case evidence inclines the mind and therefore has a cerebral effect. The trouble, for example, with subjects who persist in their ideological beliefs is not that the theoretical evidence has convinced them only cerebrally. The theoretical evidence has failed to have its usual effect—which is to say that it has failed to have a *cerebral* effect.

Nor is it the case that subjects who persist in their ideological beliefs have a merely cerebral belief that Marx is right. There are not different kinds of belief. All beliefs are the product of cerebral activity and if the subjects do not believe at heart that Marx is right, they do not believe that Marx is right in any sense, cerebral or otherwise. Further, if, when your belief defies your best evidence, we have to suppose that you also have the opposite belief in some diluted, cerebral way, we would be supposing that you are contradicting yourself. But we have seen that you are not. Your evidence is not deductive and therefore it does not entail the belief it warrants.

I can sum this up by saying that when people's beliefs fail to be affected by relevant theoretical evidence, the evidence has had no kind of impact on them and in no sense do they accept the belief which they take the evidence to warrant. It is not the case that ineffectual theoretical evidence is evidence which is appreciated intellectually or cerebrally. Nor does ineffectual theoretical evidence give rise to a special kind of belief, an intellectual belief.

The last question I want to deal with is whether my interpretation can make sense of Marx's view that ideological illusions mirror the way the world looks.

It will be remembered that in Ch. V. 1 I distinguished the interpretation of Marx whose coherence I am defending from another interpretation. The other interpretation was that ideological illusions are like perceptual illusions, the illusion that the world is as the ideology says it is being just like the illusion that a straight stick is bent in water; once exposed the ideological beliefs continue merely to seem true in the way that the stick continues to look bent. On my interpretation, by contrast, exposure makes no difference to the beliefs and they survive it. Now an advantage of the other interpretation is that it easily makes sense of Marx's claims about how the world appears, and I promised then that I would show that my interpretation could also make sense of these. Now that I have explained what my interpretation involves, namely the failure of theoretical evidence to have its usual effect, I must show how it is consistent with Marx's claims. On my interpretation, beliefs can survive superior evidence to the contrary when they are based on ubiquitous experiential evidence and the better-grounded beliefs on less vivid theoretical evidence. So the idea is that experiential evidence may have a disproportionate impact, whereas the other interpretation was that ideological illusions *are* experiences. On my interpretation the confusion is based on experience whereas on the other it is an experience. But on both interpretations we are misled by experience, and so both are consistent with Marx's claims about the world's appearing a certain way.

Incidentally, it is worth mentioning that one advantage which my interpretation has over the 'perceptual illusion' interpretation is that it makes better sense of Marx's dictum that 'The philosophers have only *interpreted* the world in various ways; the point is to *change* it'.[46] Cohen argues that there is a connection between Marx's views on reality and appearance and this dictum, the connection being that, since the world produces the ideological illusions, we will have to change the world if we are to be rid of the illusions. 'When social circumstances inevitably generate discord between thought and reality, the enemy of illusion must operate on reality, not in thought alone.'[47] But the stated reason for changing the world is much less compelling if, as Cohen thinks, 'a worker who knows Marxism . . . knows [that things] are different from what they continue to seem to be'.[48] I mentioned this claim of Cohen's earlier, that workers who are *au fait* with Marxism no longer have false beliefs. It is true that, according to Cohen, they still suffer somewhat from the

---

[46] 'Theses on Feuerbach', p. 5.
[47] Cohen, *Karl Marx's Theory of History*, p. 340.
[48] Ibid. 331.

ideology for it continues to seem true to them. But that is not so serious a symptom as to require the radical cure proposed. By contrast, there really is a reason for the radical cure, a reason to change the world, if, as I say, reading Marx is not always enough to effect a change in ideological beliefs.

4. THE INDEPENDENCE OF DESIRES FROM VALUATIONS

I have finished my discussion of how it is possible that ideological beliefs should be inseparable from economic conditions and resist the evidence that they are false. As I have already said, there is a natural extension of these claims about ideological beliefs to claims about ideological desires and it is this extension I want to deal with now. People with ideological desires have desires whose fulfilment makes them worse off, and the extension claims that even though people can come to endorse that negative judgement they will continue to be motivated by their old desires—for they too are inseparable from economic conditions. We can put this in the terminology I proposed earlier and say that the claim that belief can be passive in respect of reasoning has a partner in the claim that desire can be passive in respect of judgement—'judgement' being the term I shall use for the activity of unconditional valuing.

Now just as it seems a truism to some that beliefs must respond to what is taken to be good evidence, so it is often thought inconceivable that you should value some *x* more than anything else yet your desires fail to fall in and comply. An obvious counter-example to this is addiction, but that misses the spirit of the claim about desires and values in the same way that the occurrence of obsessional beliefs would not really be a counter-example to the popular principle about beliefs and evidence. For just as no one would deny that the beliefs of disturbed people can resist the evidence, so everyone will accept that the desires of addicts cannot be dislodged by their judgement. The right argument to put forward here, against the supposed necessary connection between desires and values, is really one I supplied in Ch. III. 4 when I argued against realism that the connection between valuation and motivation is psychological or external, not logical or internal. There is no logical guarantee that a sincere, all-out prudential valuation should motivate—some psychological input is required if action is to be the upshot.

It might seem that a good example of the failure of the psychological element to play its part is the phenomenon of weakness of will. But in fact that is not such a useful example from the point of view of Marxism, and the reason is similar to the reason why it was not all that relevant to my argument about the possibility of belief in defiance of the evidence that we can consciously allow our beliefs to surrender to a wish. The fact that a wish can consciously influence belief did not help my interpretation of Marx's claim about the tenacity of ideological illusions, just because there is no motive to believe the ideology in the case of those who are disadvantaged by it, and it had consequently to be shown that there are factors besides the obvious factor of desire which can lead people to beliefs against the weight of acknowledged evidence. The phenomenon of weakness of will cannot help a Marxist for a similar reason. When the desires of incontinent agents are too strong for their valuations, the explanation of their disproportionate strength is on the surface. The agents are tempted in one way or another. But there is nothing to be gained from the operation of *ideological* desires and so when they resist a negative valuation, the agents cannot be propelled by anything so visible. Consequently a Marxist must show that there are factors besides the highly obvious ones like the call of pleasure or the operation of a strong emotion which can explain agents' evasion of their valuations. A second difference is that there is a considerable degree of irrationality involved in weakness of will. But what happens in the case of ideological desires is less unreasonable, on account of a consideration mentioned below.

What, then, is the relevant factor in the ideological case which engages agents' wills in defiance of their judgements? A Marxist has a ready answer to this, which has to do with the fact I have already remarked on, that the ideology is fixed in all our institutions and so all our experience from early on, stamping with approval only certain goals. Certain goals and aspirations are instilled in us from such an early age and experienced as so natural that even when we read in Marx that they have no firm basis, it is very hard to stop identifying with them. Indeed, the judgement that they have no firm basis appears to come as if from someone else, an onlooker or outsider. Because the belief is not acquired experientially, it fails to have the expected impact on our desires. A psychological element necessary to make the connection between valuation and motivation is missing here.

I do not mean to imply that whenever our beliefs about what is good for us are acquired circumstantially, they cannot engage with our desires. If that were the case there would be no reason to consult experts for we could never act on their instructions. What seems to make for one difference between reading in Marx that your way of life is restricting and unprofitable and being told by, say, the doctor that your habits are debilitating, is that in the former case the issues are so highly theoretical and complicated. Also, in the ideological case the debility is not consciously felt and so the usual reason for seeking help is missing.

The reason I said that it is less unreasonable for ideological desires to resist judgement than for desires to resist a negative valuation in the weakness of will case lies precisely in the fact that agents may identify with their ideological desires. By contrast in the weakness of will case the desire is one which the agent experiences as unauthorized, and so the sense of lack of psychological integration is more profound.

It would, however, be a mistake to think that because the victims of an ideology identify with their desires, their desires cannot be alien to them. As I argued in Ch. IV. 2, the test of whether a desire is alien is not the agent's attitude to it, not whether it is experienced as alien, but rather whether it detracts from effective functioning. So although the victims of an ideology may identify with their desires, a Marxist may deny that the desires are a genuine part of the self—and say that what really *is* theirs is what *feels* to them as though it comes from an outsider, namely the judgement that they would be better off motivated in another way.

*

Marx claimed that the only way to be rid of ideological

illusions is to be rid of the social circumstances which generate them. One way to interpret that claim is to suppose that he meant that ideological beliefs can survive the impact of recognized contrary evidence. This chapter defended the coherence of that interpretation, arguing that even in the absence of a motive for the beliefs, people might persist in them in the face of acknowledged evidence supporting the hypothesis that they are false. The explanation would be the disproportionate effect of very vivid but unreliable experiential evidence on inference.

It was also argued that the same explanation could account for the phenomenon of ideological desires continuing to affect action despite an unconditional negative valuation. For agents can be pushed by their daily experience of certain aspirations and attitudes as natural in a direction different from that recommended by reason.

Conclusion

This book has been about an intriguing aspect of Marxist thought, namely its concern to expose certain 'necessary illusions'[1] about political life, to discredit agents' perceptions of political reality, and to supply an explanation for their misconceptions. At times I have used the tools of analytical philosophy to elucidate what Marxism says about these phenomena—for instance, where I explored the presuppositions of its claim that the misconceptions of members of the ruling class about their motives are explained by the economic interests they serve, and argued that their misconceptions must be motivated; or again, where I argued that Marxists ought not to talk in terms of true wants in the context of workers failing to perceive their interests. At other times I have tried to show that many of the Marxist claims can be defended philosophically, and therefore ought to be of more general interest—for instance, where I argued that Marxists are right to hold a factual and want-independent conception of interests; or again, where I tried to show that they are justified in thinking that desires can have the wrong kind of causal history. But the most general truth in this area to which Marxism points is that reason is a smaller part of ourselves than we like to think. For it is true not only of our wills, but even of our beliefs, that they can fail to synchronize with what reason tells us: just as our desires have a certain amount of autonomy *vis-à-vis* our value-judgements, so can our beliefs become dislocated from our assessment of the evidence. One of Marxism's contributions is to offer an excellent explanation of this kind of independence from reason, and that is the privileging of certain values and perceptions by experience. What is experienced as natural or inevitable acquires, as Marx

[1] This is Marx's phrase in the *Grundrisse*, p. 509.

says, 'stability'.[2] And this is an insight which carries over into non-economic areas of life too—for instance, it explains the unshakeability of certain potent images of motherhood. Indeed, that Marxist insights have this kind of resonance with experience in many areas of life has been one of the themes of this book.

[2] *Capital*, i. 80.

REFERENCES

Works by Marx and Engels

I have mostly referred to Karl Marx and Friedrich Engels, *Collected Works* (abbreviated *CW*), published in London by Lawrence and Wishart. The exceptions are the *Grundrisse*, where I refer to Martin Nicolaus's Pelican translation; the Preface to *A Contribution to the Critique of Political Economy* and 'Manifesto of the Communist Party', where I have used Marx and Engels, *Selected Works in One Volume*; and the volumes of *Capital*, where I mostly refer to the standard translations given below, but occasionally refer to the Everyman edition of *Capital*, i. Unless I state otherwise, the reference is to the standard translation.

All but one of the letters mentioned are in Marx and Engels, *Selected Correspondence*. The exception is Engels's letter to Marx of 6 August 1852, for which I have used *CW*, xxxix.

Works co-authored with Engels are preceded by an asterisk.

Unless I have indicated otherwise, passages I have italicized are also emphasized in the original.

Contribution to the Critique of Hegel's Philosophy of Law (1843), *CW*, iii (1975).

Economic and Philosophic Manuscripts (1844), *CW*, iii (1975).

Introduction to *Contribution to the Critique of Hegel's Philosophy of Law* (1844), *CW*, iii (1975).

*The Holy Family (1844), *CW*, iv (1975).

'Theses on Feuerbach' (1845), *CW*, v (1976).

**The German Ideology* (1846), *CW*, v (1976).

*'Manifesto of the Communist Party' (1848), *Selected Works in One Volume* (London: Lawrence and Wishart, 1968).

The Eighteenth Brumaire of Louis Bonaparte (1852), *CW*, xi (1979).

Grundrisse (1857–8), trans. M. Nicolaus (Harmondsworth: Penguin, 1973).

Preface to *A Contribution to the Critique of Political Economy* (1859), *Selected Works in One Volume* (London: Lawrence and Wishart, 1968).

Capital, i (1867) (London: Lawrence and Wishart, 1974; Everyman edn., London: Dent, 1974).

Capital, iii (1865) (London: Lawrence and Wishart, 1974).

**Selected Correspondence* (Moscow: Progress, 1975).

Works by Others

ACTON, H. B., *The Illusion of the Epoch* (London: Cohen and West, 1955).

ANSCOMBE, G. E. M., *Intention* (Oxford: Basil Blackwell, 1976).

ARONSON, E., *The Social Animal*, 2nd edn. (San Francisco: W. H. Freeman, 1976).

BARRY, B., *Political Argument* (London and Henley: Routledge and Kegan Paul, 1965).

BENNETT, J., *Linguistic Behaviour* (Cambridge: Cambridge University Press, 1976).

BLACKBURN, S., *Spreading the Word* (Oxford: Clarendon Press, 1984).

BOND, E. J., *Reason and Value* (Cambridge: Cambridge University Press, 1983).

BRAITHWAITE, R. B., *Scientific Explanation* (Cambridge: Cambridge University Press, 1953).

BRANDT, R. B., *A Theory of the Good and the Right* (Oxford: Clarendon Press, 1979).

CALLINICOS, A., *Marxism and Philosophy* (Oxford: Clarendon Press, 1983).

CANFIELD, J. V., and GUSTAFSON, D. F., 'Self-Deception', *Analysis*, 23 (1962).

COHEN, G. A., 'Beliefs and Roles', in J. Glover (ed.), *The Philosophy of Mind* (Oxford: Oxford University Press, 1976).

—— *Karl Marx's Theory of History: A Defence* (Oxford: Clarendon Press, 1978).

—— 'Functional Explanation: Reply to Elster', *Political Studies*, 28 (1980).

—— 'Functional Explanation, Consequence Explanation and Marxism', *Inquiry*, 25 (1982).

—— *History, Labour, and Freedom: Themes from Marx* (Oxford: Clarendon Press, 1988).

DAVIDSON, D., *Essays on Actions and Events* (Oxford: Clarendon Press, 1980).

—— 'Paradoxes of Irrationality', in R. Wollheim and J. Hopkins (eds.), *Philosophical Essays on Freud* (Cambridge: Cambridge University Press, 1982).

—— 'Deception and Division', in E. Lepore and B. McLaughlin (eds.), *Actions and Events* (New York: Basil Blackwell, 1985).

DEUTSCHER, I., *Marxism in Our Time* (London: Jonathan Cape, 1972).

ELSTER, J., 'Cohen on Marx's Theory of History', *Political Studies*, 28 (1980).

—— *Sour Grapes* (Cambridge: Cambridge University Press, 1983).

—— *Making Sense of Marx* (Cambridge: Cambridge University Press, 1985).

—— *An Introduction to Karl Marx* (Cambridge: Cambridge University Press, 1986).

EWEN, S., *Captains of Consciousness* (New York: McGraw-Hill, 1976).

FANON, F., *Black Skin White Masks* (Frogmore: Paladin, 1970).

FEINBERG, J. C., 'Harm and Self-Interest', in *Rights, Justice and the Bounds of Liberty* (New Jersey: Princeton University Press, 1980).

FLEMING, P. A., 'The Moral Status of Deprogramming', *Journal of Applied Philosophy*, 6 (1989).

FRANKFURT, H., 'Freedom of the Will and the Concept of a Person', *Journal of Philosophy*, 68 (1971).

FREEDMAN, J. L., SEARS, D. O., and CARLSMITH, J. M. (eds.), *Social Psychology* (New Jersey: Prentice-Hall, 1981).

FREUD, S., *Complete Psychological Works of Sigmund Freud*, Standard Edition (London, 1953–73).

GARDINER, P., 'Error, Faith, and Self-Deception', in J. Glover (ed.), *The Philosophy of Mind* (Oxford: Oxford University Press, 1976).

GEUSS, R., *The Idea of a Critical Theory* (Cambridge: Cambridge University Press, 1981).

GOMBRICH, E. H., *Art and Illusion*, 2nd edn. (London: Phaidon Press, 1962).

GORDIMER, N., *The Conservationist* (London: Jonathan Cape, 1974).

GRICE, G. R., 'Motive and Reason', in J. Raz (ed.), *Practical Reasoning* (Oxford: Oxford University Press, 1978).

GRIFFIN, J., 'Are There Incommensurable Values?', *Philosophy and Public Affairs*, 7 (1977).

GRIMSHAW, J., 'Autonomy and Identity in Feminist Thinking', in M. Griffiths and M. Whitford (eds.), *Feminist Perspectives in Philosophy* (London: Macmillan, 1988).

HAMPSHIRE, S., 'Morality and Convention', in A. Sen and B. Williams (eds.), *Utilitarianism and Beyond* (Cambridge: Cambridge University Press, 1982).

HARE, R. M., *Freedom and Reason* (Oxford: Oxford University Press, 1963).

HARSANYI, J., 'Morality and the Theory of Rational Behaviour', in A. Sen and B. Williams (eds.), *Utilitarianism and Beyond* (Cambridge: Cambridge University Press, 1982).

HEGEL, G. W. F., *Philosophy of Right*, trans. T. M. Knox (Oxford: Oxford University Press, 1973).

HONDERICH, T., 'Against Teleological Historical Materialism', *Inquiry*, 25 (1982).

HUME, D., *A Treatise of Human Nature*, ed. L. A. Selby-Bigge (Oxford: Clarendon Press, 1973).

KANT, I., *The Groundwork of the Metaphysic of Morals*, trans. by H. J. Paton as *The Moral Law* (London: Hutchinson, 1972).

LEAR, J., 'Moral Objectivity', in S. C. Brown (ed.), *Objectivity and Cultural Divergence, Royal Institute of Philosophy Lectures*, xvii (Cambridge: Cambridge University Press, 1984).

LERNER, M. J., 'The desire for justice and reactions to victims', in J. Macaulay and L. Berkowitz (eds.), *Altruism and Helping Behaviour* (New York: Academic Press, 1970).

LIFTON, R. J., *Thought Reform and the Psychology of Totalism* (London: Victor Gollancz, 1962).

LUKÁCS, G., *History and Class Consciousness* (London: Merlin Press, 1971).

LUKES, S., 'Can the Base be Distinguished from the Superstructure', in D. Miller and L. Siedentop (eds.), *The Nature of Political Theory* (Oxford: Clarendon Press, 1983).

—— *Marxism and Morality* (Oxford: Clarendon Press, 1985).

MCCARNEY, J., *The Real World of Ideology* (Sussex: Harvester Press, 1980).

MCDOWELL, J., 'Are Moral Requirements Hypothetical Imperatives?', *Proceedings of the Aristotelian Society*, suppl. vol. 52 (1978).

MACKIE, J. L., *Ethics* (Harmondsworth: Penguin, 1977).

MCLELLAN, D., *The Young Hegelians and Karl Marx* (London: Macmillan, 1969).

—— *Ideology* (Milton Keynes: Open University Press, 1986).

MAILER, N., *Tough Guys Don't Dance* (London: Sphere Books, 1984).

MARCUSE, H., *One-Dimensional Man* (London: Routledge and Kegan Paul, 1964).

MELE, A. R., *Irrationality* (New York and Oxford: Oxford University Press, 1987).

MILL, J. S., *On Liberty* in *Utilitarianism, On Liberty, Essay on Bentham*, ed. M. Warnock (London: Collins/Fontana, 1962).

MILLER, D., 'Ideology and the Problem of False Consciousness', *Political Studies*, 20 (1972).

MILLER, R. W., *Analyzing Marx: Morality, Power, and History* (Princeton: Princeton University Press, 1984).

NAGEL, T., *The Possibility of Altruism* (Oxford: Clarendon Press, 1970).

—— 'Death', in *Mortal Questions* (Cambridge: Cambridge University Press, 1979).

NISBETT, R., *et al.*, 'Popular induction: Information is not necessarily informative', in D. Kahneman, *et al.*, (eds.), *Judgment under uncertainty: Heuristics and biases* (Cambridge: Cambridge University Press, 1982).

NISBETT, R., and ROSS, L., *Human Inference: Strategies and Shortcomings of Social Judgment* (New Jersey: Prentice-Hall, 1980).

OPIE, I., and OPIE, P., *The Classic Fairy Tales* (London: Granada, 1980).

ORWELL, G., 'Politics and the English Language', in D. Lodge (ed.), *20th Century Literary Criticism* (London: Longman, 1972).

PACKARD, V., *The Hidden Persuaders* (Harmondsworth: Penguin, 1960).

PARFIT, D., *Reasons and Persons* (Oxford: Clarendon Press, 1984).

PEARS, D., *Questions in the Philosophy of Mind* (London: Duckworth, 1975).

—— 'Motivated Irrationality, Freudian Theory and Cognitive Dissonance', in R. Wollheim and J. Hopkins (eds.), *Philosophical Essays on Freud* (Cambridge: Cambridge University Press, 1982).

—— *Motivated Irrationality* (Oxford: Clarendon Press, 1984).

PLAMENATZ, J., *Man and Society,* ii (London: Longmans, 1963).

PRICE, H. H., *Belief* (London: George Allen and Unwin, 1969).

REZNEK, L., *The Nature of Disease* (London and New York: Routledge and Kegan Paul, 1987).

ROUSSEAU, J. J., *The Social Contract and Discourses* (London: Dent, 1973).

RUSSELL, B., *The Analysis of Mind* (London: George Allen and Unwin, 1921).

RUSSELL, K., 'Science and Ideology: Critical comments on John Mepham's article', in J. Mepham and D-H. Ruben (eds.), *Issues in Marxist Philosophy,* iii (Sussex: Harvester Press, 1979).

SACKS, O., *The Man who Mistook his Wife for a Hat* (London: Duckworth, 1985).

SARTRE, J. P., *Being and Nothingness*, trans. H. E. Barnes (New York: Philosophical Library, 1956).

SEIGEL, J., *Marx's Fate* (Princeton: Princeton University Press, 1978).

SIEGLER, F. A., 'Demos on Lying to Oneself', *Journal of Philosophy,* 59 (1962).

SKINNER, Q., 'Language and Social Change', in L. Michaels and C. Ricks (eds.), *The State of the Language* (Berkeley and Los Angeles: University of California Press, 1980).

SMITH, M., 'The Humean Theory of Motivation', *Mind,* 96 (1987).

STRAWSON, G., *Freedom and Belief* (Oxford: Clarendon Press, 1986).

TAYLOR, C., *The Explanation of Behaviour* (London and Henley: Routledge and Kegan Paul, 1964).

—— 'Teleological Explanation: A Reply to Denis Noble', *Analysis,* 27 (1966–7).

—— 'What's Wrong with Negative Liberty?', in A. Ryan (ed.), *The Idea of Freedom* (Oxford: Oxford University Press, 1979).

THOMPSON, J. B., *Studies in the Theory of Ideology* (Cambridge: Polity Press, 1984).

WAUGH, E., *Brideshead Revisited* (London: Heinemann, 1977).

WELDON, F., *Praxis* (Great Britain: Hodder and Stoughton, 1978).

WIGGINS, D., 'Truth, Invention, and the Meaning of Life', *Proceedings of the British Academy,* 62 (1976).

WIGGINS, D., 'Claims of Need', in *Needs, Values and Truth* (Oxford: Blackwell, 1987).

WILLIAMS, B., *Morality* (Harmondsworth, Penguin, 1972).

—— 'Deciding to Believe', in *Problems of the Self* (Cambridge: Cambridge University Press, 1973).

—— *Descartes: The Project of Pure Enquiry* (Harmondsworth, Penguin, 1978).

—— 'Internal and External Reasons', in R. Harrison (ed.), *Rational Action* (Cambridge: Cambridge University Press, 1979).

WINNICOTT, D., *The Maturational Processes and the Facilitating Environment* (London: The Hogarth Press and the Institute of Psycho-Analysis, 1965).

WITTGENSTEIN, L., *Philosophical Investigations*, trans. G. E. M. Anscombe (Oxford: Blackwell, 1976).

WOLLHEIM, R., 'Needs, Desires and Moral Turpitude', in *Nature and Conduct, Royal Institute of Philosophy Lectures*, viii (London: Macmillan, 1975).

WOOD, A., *Karl Marx* (London, Boston and Henley: Routledge and Kegan Paul, 1981).

WRIGHT, L., *Teleological Explanations* (Berkeley: University of California Press, 1976).

INDEX

actions:
  whether non-cognitive states are
    necessary for 80-1, 85, 86,
    97-9, 102, 103-4, 105
  reasons and, *see* reasons for
    actions
Acton, H. B. 18-26 *passim*
adaptability of purposive behaviour
  60-1
addiction 120, 165
advertising 7, 133, 138, 139
all-things-considered judgements
  96, 101
animal beliefs 39, 48
animal social organization 45
Anscombe, G. E. M. 125
appearances, misleading 3, 4, 148-9
  see also belief(s); experience, and;
    illusions, and

'backwards causation' 32
Barry, B. 78 n.
base:
  as necessity of life 26-7
  relationship to superstructure
    according to Engels 27-9
  relationship to superstructure
    causally construed 18-26
  superstructure explained by
    stabilizing effect on 29-33
  see also economic relations
belief-disposing factors 152, 158-9
belief(s):
  whether action-guiding or not, *see*
    actions, whether non-cognitive
    states are necessary for
  aim at truth 63 n., 125-7, 131
  automatic response to desires 9,
    39-40, 43, 56-9, 62, 68, 69, 111
  compartmentalization of 57
  economic benefits explain 6, 8,
    11, 29-30, 34, 40, 41-2, 130

experience and 5, 10, 14, 160-2,
  164, 166-8; *see also* appearances,
  misleading
history of 8-9, 11, 135-6
illusions and 146-51
irrational causation of 11, 46,
  56-7, 111, 131, 136
motivated 13, 36-40, 43-4, 61-8,
  69, 90
about motives 4, 5-6, 14-15, 34-6,
  48-54, 67-8; *see also*
  rationalization
non-rational causation of 11, 43,
  44-8, 55
passivity in respect of reasoning
  157-8, 165, 169; *see also* belief(s),
  survive contrary evidence
passivity in respect of the will
  157
passivity of other mental
  phenomena in respect of 157
programmed 38-9, 43, 44-5, 50,
  68; *see also* innateness
  hypothesis
rational causation of 11, 46
role in history 54-5
survival value of 8, 38-9, 48
survive contrary evidence 10,
  57-8, 126-7, 151-2, 155-6, 158,
  165, 168; *see also* belief(s),
  passivity in respect of
  reasoning
usefulness of 6, 8, 11, 13, 24,
  29-30, 34-40, 49 *see also*
  ideology
Bennett, J. 32
Black Consciousness 73
Blackburn, S. 76
Bond, E. J. 97-8
Braithwaite, R. B. 60
Brandt, R. 123-4

Callinicos, A. 12
Calvinism 47
Canfield, J. V. 64
capitalism 3, 8, 47, 70, 107, 131, 139,
    145, 160
character 136–7, 139–40, 141
    see also personality
class 17
class consciousness 71–2, 80
    absence in working class of 7,
      132–5
cognitive dissonance 53, 132–3
Cohen, G. A. 17 n, 19, 22–3, 27,
      29–32, 41, 147, 164
coincidental benefits 37–8, 40, 41–2,
      132–3
'cold' errors 37
colonial values 7
commodities 4, 146, 148
commodity fetishism 148–9, 150,
      161
communism 108
conditioned beliefs 136
conditioned desires 123, 134–6,
      138–40
conditioning 9, 15, 123, 129, 134–6,
      138–42
consciousness:
    of existence of motive to believe
      67–8
    'irrelevance' to history 54
    of influence of desire on belief
      56–9
    moulding of working-class 135
consequence explanations 31, 33,
      54
conspiracy hypothesis 133–4
contradictory beliefs 57, 64–5, 67
Corn Laws 34
cults 138–9

Darwinism 31–2, 40–1
Davidson, D. 11, 21, 25, 46, 56 n., 66,
      109
'debriefing' 154, 155, 159
deliberation 56, 61–2
desire(s):
    as action-disposing 80, 97–8, 109

aim at the good 124–7
alien 142–5, 167
causation of 8, 9, 54–5, 95, 130–5,
      145
    economic benefits explain 8, 9,
      130–1
    freedom reduced by 140–5
    global effect of conditioning on
      140
    identification with 143, 144, 167
    inappropriate 7, 8, 9, 70–3, 89,
      128–9, 130
    intentionality of 78
    interests and, *see* interest(s),
      whether want-based or
      want-independent
    irresistible 122–3
    manipulation of 137–9
    misidentification of 87–94
    as necessary for action, *see* actions,
      (whether non-cognitive states
      are necessary for as necessary
      to explain how interest served
      by misperception of motives
      48–55, 68
    norm for 126
    passivity in respect of judgement
      165–7; *see also* desire(s), survive
      negative valuation
    pathological 120
    role in history 54–5
    satisfaction vs. fulfilment 91
    survive negative valuation 10,
      103–4, 126, 128–9, 165–8; *see also*
      desire(s), passivity in respect of
      judgement
    'true', *see* true wants
    unextinguishable 123–4
    universal 124
    usefulness of 7, 8, 130
determinism:
    economic 54
    and freedom 145
    technological 17 n
Deutscher, I. 162
divided mind 13, 66, 67
doxastic incontinence 152 n
duties, *see* rights

economic powers 23, 24, 29
economic relations 2–3, 17–33,
54–5, 130–4
see also base
economic structure, *see* economic
relations
Elster, J. 17 n., 41, 53, 132, 134
emotions 8, 50, 103, 133, 144
Engels, F. 1, 2, 4, 5, 6, 27–8, 34, 36,
62, 134
evidence:
beliefs can resist, *see* belief(s),
survive contrary evidence
derogation of the source of 155
experiential vs. theoretical 10,
160–4, 168, 169–70
failure to register 155–6
rejection of 155
experiments, psychological 152–6,
158–9
exploitation 8
concealed 24, 149
and self-image 49, 54, 56, 133

face-to-face vs. statistical
information 153, 155
false hunger and thirst 95
false self 137
Feinberg, J. 116, 118–19
feminism 7, 15, 73, 129, 139
Feuerbach, L. 1, 2
forces of production, *see* productive
forces
Frankfurt, H. 142–3
free will 142–3
freedom:
appearance of under capitalism
4, 148, 160
ideological desires restrict 140–5
Marxist concept of 141
neurological disorders and 143–4
psychological disorders and
144–5
Freud, S. 66, 89, 90–1, 93, 94, 162
functional explanations 31–2
function-statements 32

Gardiner, P. 63

genetic fallacy 13–14
Geuss, R. 12–13
Gombrich, E. H. 157
good for people, what is, *see*
interests
good life 87
interests and 124, 127–8
moral life and 116
universality of 107–9
Gordimer, N. 35
Gramsci, A. 134–5
Grice, G. R. 99–103, 109–10
Griffin, J. 93
Grimshaw, J. 129
Gustafson, D. F. 64

Hampshire, S. 123
Hare, R. M. 114
Harsanyi, J. 88–9
Hegel, G. W. F. 1, 87
Heidegger, M. 141
hierarchical mentality 45
historical materialism, *see* base
Hobbes, T. 3, 96
Honderich, T. 28, 54
human interests 107–9, 131
human nature 107–9, 145
Hume, D. 22, 79, 81, 97–8, 104, 105
Hutcheson, F. 103

ideology:
distorting effect of 104, 166–7
economic structure and 2–3,
17–33
entrenchment of economic
relations by 8, 24, 29–30, 134–5
explained by its usefulness 8,
29–33
falsity of ideological beliefs 4–5,
11–14, 161
fixed in institutions 10, 128–9,
160–2, 166–8, 169–70
influence on attitudes to desires
143
inseparable from economy 4, 10,
150, 165
see also belief(s); illusions

illusions:
  cognitive 150
  ideological 6–7, 34, 49–50, 62,
    146–50, 156, 160–1, 163–4, 167–8
  perceptual 149, 150, 151, 157,
    163–4
  see also appearances, misleading;
    ideology
images of women 129
imagination 157
improvisation and purposive
  behaviour 60–1
innateness hypothesis 44–7
  see also belief(s), programmed
intellectual incompetence and
  mistakes about motives 36–7
intention 59, 63, 65, 68, 69
interest(s):
  choices and 114
  whether factual or not 9, 14–15,
    73–5, 76–7, 79, 82–4, 86, 104–6,
    124, 127; *see also*
    non-cognitivism
  hedonistic conception of 114–16,
    119
  judgements about, *see* prudential
    judgements
  mistakes about, *see* desire(s),
    inappropriate
  'real' 7, 14–15
  whether universal or not 107–9,
    122–3
  virtue and 116–17, 118, 120, 126
  whether want-based or
    want-independent 9, 15, 49,
    73–5, 76–9, 80, 81, 82–6, 113–14,
    116–24
  see also prudential
    valuations/judgements
interest-based wants 80, 83–4
  see also true wants

justice, desire for 52–3

Kant, I. 118

labour 4, 24, 146–7, 148, 149, 160
  division of 107–8

labour power 3–4, 19, 23, 146, 149
Lamarck, J.-B. 41
Lear, J. 112–13, 121
legal relations and economic
  relations, *see* base
Lenin, V. I. 71, 72
Lifton, R. 138
Lukács, G. 71, 72, 80, 96, 160–1
Lukes, S. 23 n.

McCarney, J. 12 n.
McDowell, J. 98, 99, 101, 102, 103
Mailer, N. 10
Malthus, T. R. 6
Marcuse, H. 7, 72, 130, 139, 143
Marx, K.:
  on capitalism as 'enchanted'
    world 3–4, 14, 148–9, 160–1
  on changing the world 164
  on freedom 141
  on human interests, human
    nature, and the good life
    107–8, 124, 131, 145
  on idealism 5
  on ideology 1–4, 24, 146
  on illusions of the ruling class 6,
    15, 34, 62
  on 'imaginary appetites' 70, 87,
    90–1
  on the intellectual dominance of
    the ruling class 7, 134
  on the interests of the proletariat
    15
  on materialist conception of
    history 2–3, 17, 40
  on myths and legends 59
  on the nature of relations of
    production 19
  on the need for a 'fatiguing climb'
    162
  on the need to produce 26–7
  on obsessive consumption 70–1
  on the role of human agency in
    history 54–5
  on state of nature theory 3
  on the tenacity of our
    understandings of social life 4,
    128, 146–7, 150, 156, 169–70

meaning of life 73–4
Mele, A. 66 n., 152 n
mental causation, *see* belief(s),
    irrational causation of; belief(s),
    rational causation of
Mill, J. S. 78, 88, 136–7, 139–40
Miller, R. 17 n.
moral life and good life 116
moral motives 102–3, 118–19, 120,
    126
moral realism 82, 96
morality and economic relations, *see*
    base
morality vs. moral judgements 75–6
motivation, *see* actions; reasons for
    actions

Nagel, T. 81 n., 103, 115
needs:
    biological 105–6, 108, 123
    crude and human 70–1, 108
    desires and 121 n.
    'false' 7, 70, 130
    manipulation of 72
    satisfaction and 93
Newman, J. H. 151
Nietzsche, F. 120, 133
Nisbett, R. 37
non-cognitivism 74–6, 105
    see also interest(s), whether factual
    or not non-mental casuation,
    see belief(s), non-rational
    causation of

Orwell, G. 58–9

Pangloss 30, 41
Parfit, D. 119
Pears, D. 38, 50, 56–7, 64–5, 66, 67,
    68 n., 93, 158
personality 137, 143–5
    see also character
Plamenatz, J. 19–26 *passim*
Plato 87, 116–17, 118, 120
political relations and economic
    relations, *see* base
Price, H. H. 147
prima-facie judgements 96, 101

productive forces 2, 3, 17
prudential valuations/
    judgements:
    whether expressions of belief or
    of desire, *see* interest(s), whether
    factual or not
    independence of desires from, *see*
    desire(s), survive negative
    valuation
    whether necessarily practical
    80–1, 82, 83–4, 85–6, 96–104,
    105
    relationship to reasons for action
    98, 99, 100, 109, 110
    see also interest(s)
psychological egoism 96, 101
purposive behaviour 59–61
purposive promotion of belief, *see*
    belief(s), motivated

racist and sexist stereotypes 161,
    162
rationalization 6, 8, 9, 38, 44, 47, 53,
    54, 55, 56, 59, 130–1, 133
    see also belief(s), about motives
realist version of Marxism 82, 84,
    85–6, 96–104, 128
reasons for actions:
    as causes of actions 21, 22
    whether cognitions are enough to
    yield 98, 99, 100, 109, 110
    external and internal 111–13
    whether necessarily motivating
    100, 109
    not necessarily rational 111–13
    objective 112–13
reductionism 84, 85–6, 106
relations of production, *see*
    economic relations
Reznek, L. 105
rights (and duties) 19–21, 23, 29
Ross, L. 37
Rousseau, J. J. 87, 94, 95, 141–2
Russell, B. 91, 92
Russell, K. 5 n.

Sacks, O. 143, 144
Sartre, J. P. 63, 64

Seigel, J. 5 n.
self-deception 63–8
Siegler, F. A. 64
Skinner, Q. 34–5
Smith, M. 81 n.
Strawson, G. 141 n.
subjectivism 82, 84, 85, 86, 104–5,
    113
sub-system, mental, *see* divided mind
superstructure, *see* base

Taylor, C. 21 n., 142, 144
Taylor, R. 73–4
Tourette's syndrome 143–4
true wants 15, 79–80, 84, 85, 86,
    87–95
    see also interest-based wants

unconscious metal processes 39–40,
    56, 66–8, 89, 90–1

utilitarianism 114

vanity 51
Voltaire 30

Waugh, E. 35–6
weakness of will 111, 166, 167
Webb, B. 35
Weber, M. 47
Weldon, F. 106
well-being 9, 120–1, 125–6
Wiggins, D. 73–5, 76–7, 108, 121 n.,
    127
will-disposing factors 166–7
Williams, B. 63 n., 75, 111–12, 127,
    136, 157
Wittgenstein, L. 157
Wollheim, R. 121
Wood, A. 12
Wright, L. 32